FISHERS

OF

MEN

APOSTLES OF THE MODERN AGE

JOHN M. JANARO

TRINITY COMMUNICATIONS
MANASSAS, VIRGINIA

ISBN 0-937495-05-0

DEDICATION

This book is dedicated to all the faithful and devoted priests who serve the Church of Jesus Christ in the United States of America. To these "Apostles of the Modern Age", be they young or old, famous or unknown, I offer this work as a recognition of the irreplaceable ministry of each of them, and in profound gratitude for their leadership and sacrifice.

ACKNOWLEDGEMENTS

This book would not have been possible without the efforts and cooperation of several people. In this regard I would like to thank three priests in particular, who were instrumental in assisting us—Fr. John A. Hardon, Fr. Robert J. Fox, and Fr. Kenneth Baker. I also wish to acknowledge my brothers and sisters in the Lord who contributed to the progress and development of the work: Dr. Jeffrey A. Mirus, for conceiving and directing the whole project; Ann McOsker Francis, for production and correction of the manuscript; Jeanette O'Connor, for typing substantial portions of the manuscript; Irene Furtado and Barbara Mirus, for their careful proofreading; Patrick Diemer, for his artwork; and Matthew Gelis, for his assistance and consultation in the use of the word processor.

Finally I would especially like to mention the angel whom the Lord has given me as my guardian and guide, whose presence and inspiration continually brought to mind the reality of the Word made flesh, and consoled me during many lonely hours on the road.

Vocations Support Program

Fishers of Men is published in conjunction with Trinity Communications' special Vocations Support Program. Through this program, young men considering a vocation to the priesthood can receive advice, encouragement, free materials and even spiritual formation through Trinity Communications and its Spiritual Director, Fr. Robert J. Fox.

Those interested should contact Trinity Communications for a free booklet by Fr. Fox entitled *Guidance for Future Priests*. See page 200 (last page) of this book for details.

Basis for Selection for Inclusion in this Book

The priests included in this work were selected by the publisher in consultation with a committee of clerical and lay advisors. Each candidate had to meet four criteria. He had to be: a)characterized, in the view of the committee, by deep spirituality, leadership in the apostolate, and fidelity to the Magisterium of the Church; b)well-known at least to some members of the committee; c)willing to participate; d)available for extensive interviews during the Summer of 1986. In addition, the publisher has sought diversity of ministry and variety of geographical location.

This book is intended neither as a collection of the ten *best* priests in the United States (our candidates agreed to be included only if it were *not* such a collection) nor as an effort to endorse or condemn any diocese or religious order. The profiles included here are rather intended to be representative of many other faithful priests around the country, in the hope that such a representation may encourage all priests, inspire lay people, and foster vocations among the young.

Publisher's Foreword

Fishers of Men has an interesting history. It began when, in the wake of the 1985 Extraordinary Synod, we began to plan potential books which would *exemplify* the renewal for which the Pope had called, books that could therefore inspire readers to even greater effort in renewing the Church as a whole. After some reflection, it seemed that the best way to do this might be to tell the stories of a series of American priests whose ministries were characterized by deep spirituality, leadership in the apostolate, and fidelity to the Magisterium of the Church. In consultation with Trinity's Spiritual Director, Fr. Robert Fox, and with Frs. John Hardon and Kenneth Baker, S.J., we began to make concrete plans.

And what plans! Before long we saw the impact such a book could have not only on the Catholic faithful and the many good priests who serve them, but specifically on young men who might be more likely to pursue vocations to the priesthood with examples like these to follow. And if we were able to inspire the young men, we might also answer their initial questions about their vocations. And if we were to answer questions, we might at least offer opportunities for spiritual formation and advice on finding good seminaries. Thus, the Trinity Communications Vocations Support Program was born, under the spiritual direction of Fr. Fox (see details on page 200).

It remained to find an author for *Fishers of Men*. John Janaro's name surfaced almost immediately. Here was a young, well-formed Christendom College graduate, a man pursuing advanced theological studies with a wisdom far beyond his years, a responsible analyst of the current scene, and a brilliant writer. Was he available?

He was. Commissioned to do the work in May of 1986,

Janaro spent his summer travelling to visit priests all over the country, spending days with each candidate, interviewing and observing, photographing and taping, taking notes, distilling everything, and writing the chapters. It was, he says, an exhilarating spiritual experience. We think he communicates that experience here.

But the story of this book would still be incomplete without one personal note, a note about my private devotion to my guardian angel. On very rare occasions I have been blessed with a rapid series of insights when I have attempted to speak to my angel in prayer, insights which amount to a sort of instantaneous conversation in the mind. I make no pretense of asserting the validity of these insights as authentic supernatural experiences, but one sudden notion in connection with this book may be worth offering just the same.

I was out on a long night walk, a rosary walk, and I had drifted into prayerful reflection on some of the hard times I had faced in certain apostolates over the years. I remember that my guardian angel seemed particularly near. Mentally noting how I had always (at least in the bad times) tried to commend these apostolates to his attention, I asked him whether it was he who had carried the apostolates through when they seemed unable to go on. "Yes," (he seemed to say), "it was."

But then (I said in my mind), I should like to put another question. If you carried the apostolates in their hard times, is it therefore true that you also carried *me* when I thought I could not go on?

"Carry *you*?" (he seemed to reply). "In God's name, no. It was the *priests* who carried *you*."

It was an answer I did not in the least expect, and yet it seems almost certainly true. *Fishers of Men*, then, will thank the priests.

Jeffrey A. Mirus
October 14, 1986

Table of Contents

Introduction

The new People of God, born of an everlasting covenant in Christ Jesus, journey along the footpaths of the world through suffering and strife on their pilgrimage to the Father. In Christ they are raised up, their lives joined to His offering of Himself, an offering that constitutes their purpose and mission as a People, a Love that binds them, penetrates them, and sets them aflame.

"*. . . one Spirit was given to us all to drink*" (1 Cor 12:13). This mission—this love—flows from the Heart of Jesus Christ crucified, and passes through his ministers who represent each day that New Covenant, manifesting the presence and power of the Lord. The union between the priest and his people is continually renewed on the path of pilgrimage—Christ the shepherd directs and nourishes the flock in the mission of the priesthood, and the priest builds up and serves the body of Christ in his responsiveness to the faithful.

Thus the entire Church proclaims the Gospel not simply by speaking about Jesus but more fundamentally by living the very mystery of the redemption, united throughout the ages to the Son of Man as He offers Himself to the Father. The mission of the priesthood is rooted in the very life of the Church; the priest takes the contents of his service—the particular times, places, and the Christian people in his care—and draws them into the redemptive act of Jesus Christ. Therefore the substance of priestly ministry is nothing less than the transformation of the lives of God's people into the obedience of Christ to the Father. *"I tell you most solemnly, whoever believes in me will perform the same works as I do myself"* (John 14:12).

During the present time it is important to reflect upon the fundamental significance of the Catholic priesthood. The faithful Christian of today is painfully aware of what has been called a crisis of faith. The Church appears to be in great turmoil, struggling with the rebelliousness of the world that does not know the Son of God, a rebellion that seems to have infected some of her own members. The crisis of faith corresponds to a crisis of vocations to the priesthood. Today there are fewer men being ordained to the priesthood than in previous times, and many of those who are already priests have lost the sense of their calling. People say that Catholicism is weak—that perhaps it is *dying*—and the faithful themselves often wonder, "what is happening to the Church?"

". . . because unless I go, the Advocate will not come to you" (John 16:7). In the midst of all these difficulties, however, the Church continues to focus upon renewal, and has hoped and prayed for strength of faith, firmness of purpose, and clarity of mission. The Church seeks once again the vitality of Pentecost, a new outpouring of the Holy Spirit. The hope of the Second Vatican Council, and the core of its message, is a call to the whole Church to receive the Holy Spirit and to go forth with a renewed dedication to the service of humanity.

When we reflect upon the union of the Church with Christ, we realize that this kind of renewal cannot *fail*; the tensions and fashions of the day cannot *prevent Christ from going to the Father*. And it is from Christ's obedience that the Spirit is sent; it is from the Cross—through His pierced Heart—that redemption flows. Thus the Church today—abandoned and alone, appearing weak and afflicted, betrayed by those who were once in her bosom, neglected by others who have fled her in fear and confusion, mocked by passers-by, and all the while "thirsting" for the salvation of all men—is perhaps closer in her conformity to Jesus, in her penetration of the very reality of His redemptive sacrifice, than ever before in her pilgrimage upon this earth.

The presence of suffering and crisis, then, should not conceal the profound renewal of the Church and the life-giving presence of the Holy Spirit from those who have faith. For the People of God share in the mystery of *a crucified Christ*, one who is *madness* to those who do not believe *"but to those who have been called . . . a Christ who is the power and the wisdom of God"* (1 Cor 1:23-24). And if we believe that the Church today is drawing more closely to her source in the mystery of the redemption, we should expect to find a hidden strength in the priestly ministry that is so central to the union of Christ and His Church.

This belief and this expectation constitute the spirit in which this book is written. It is a book about the priesthood as it exists today in the churches in the United States, and it seeks to demonstrate the manner in which the Holy Spirit has prepared and is now bringing about the renewal of priestly life. It details the lives of ten men who have embraced the service of the priesthood with an attitude of fidelity to the Gospel of Jesus Christ. These men represent the body of dedicated priests all across the country, many of whom I have met and spoken with in the course of putting this book together. Some of the priests in this book are easily recognized as leaders in the American Catholic community, while others perhaps are less well known. Their visible contributions to the growth of the Church also vary, and these men have not been chosen because they *stand out* from the rest, or because they are somehow "more significant" than their brother priests. This is *not* a book about the ten *best* priests in America—as though anyone could possibly draw up such a list. Rather it is a book that seeks to show how the Spirit is renewing the Church in the midst of crisis, and to reveal this renewal by presenting profiles of different priests exercising their ministry in various situations—a ministry that proceeds in each case from a vocation that is, as we know, a work of the Holy Spirit.

Therefore, since the vocation to the priesthood is a concrete thing that always takes shape in particular times and places, these profiles detail the lives of certain persons. Nevertheless honor or particular recognition was not a criterion in selecting the priests for this book. The gift of the priestly vocation and its central importance in the Church, as well as the reality of the renewal that God has willed for her in these times, clearly indicate that any faithful priest could serve as an example of the Holy Spirit working within the Church. Indeed this book bears witness to that fact; the priests who appear within these pages were determined by a variety of factors including availability for extensive interview, willingness to participate in the project, considerations of regional diversity, and the very variety of their priestly service. The only *central* consideration in their selection was that they all be priests and they all be faithful to the Gospel and committed to the Church. It is hoped that these profiles will reveal that every priest who possesses this commitment is an instrument of the Lord for the renewal of His Body.

St. John the Evangelist concludes his Gospel by proclaiming that if all the works of Jesus were written down *"the world itself, I suppose, would not hold all the books that would have to be written"* (John 21:25). No doubt this holds true today, and this book can only seek to present a small part of the depth of Christ's presence and action in the Church in America.

It is my sincere hope that *Fishers of Men* will contribute to a greater awareness of this Divine presence. I hope that all who believe in Jesus Christ will see in these profiles the pivotal role of the ordained priesthood in vivifying the whole Church, and will thus become more conscious of the priestly vocation as the instrument through which Jesus unites each of the faithful, whom He calls to the fullness of Christian life, to His own life. I also hope that those who are considering the priesthood themselves will see in these examples the challenge and the necessity of the Catholic priesthood in these times when the Church draws particularly close to the essence of her conformity to the Son of Man in His act of redeeming the world, a conformity that is the very heart and purpose of the priestly life. *"I commissioned you to go out and to bear fruit, fruit that will last"* (John 15:16).

I.
Father Robert J. Fox

The sun glimmers on the horizon, shedding its golden hue across the fields that stretch as far as the eye can see. Birds begin to sing, fireflies blink, and the shadows of a small town become long and faded as its skyline melts into silhouette. The shapes of farmhouses and grain bins draw into a cluster around a prominent water tower that announces its identity: Alexandria, South Dakota. Somewhat removed from the water tower another structure rises above the landscape—it is the steeple of St. Mary of Mercy Catholic Church.

"Blessed are the meek, for they shall inherit the earth" (Mt. 5:5). The people of this place are straightforward and practical; they bring forth their livelihood each day from what nature—aided by their own good sense—raises out of the ground. They grin and grip your hand with firmness and warmth; and you feel as though they are honestly glad to meet you. Six hundred of these people inhabit Alexandria, just enough to give them their own exit on interstate 90. And on this particular evening one of them is out for a walk; by his stature and the length of his stride he is unmistakably a farmer, but his clothes display that he is a laborer in another harvest. As he strolls along he stops to talk to passers-by, or perhaps to wave to some-

one across the road. People respond with respect and affection; everyone seems to know him, indeed to know him as a personal friend. Especially the children. . . .

"Hi, Father Fox," the head of a little girl pokes out from around a doorway. She wears a smile as they exchange some small conversation; she is introducing her cousins, two small children that Fr. Fox does not yet know. But he will.

The youth of America are bombarded with things that attempt to make a claim on their hearts. In the midst of this there is one man who uses his every ability to offer them his heart. Fr. Robert J. Fox has a mission to young people, and a message to proclaim: there is another way to live, God's way. In order to say this, however, he must demonstrate that way in his own life. This demonstration has taken many forms, as author and journalist, as television personality, as leader in the World Apostolate of Fatima. In all, however, he is priest, and he touches the lives of his people—particularly young people—by living the life of Jesus, human in its tenderness and intimacy, divine in the fact that it knows no limit.

Fr. Fox has a truly international public that includes Cardinals and members of the Roman Curia. Yet they have not drawn him out of his simplicity of life and its roots in the fields and farms of South Dakota. On the contrary he has drawn them into his simple vision, a vision of the Mystical Body of Christ, the Christ who has known hard work, suffering, and great love.

Such characteristics filled the household of Aloysius and Susie Emma Fox, who ran a farm near Watertown, S.D. They were devout people, for whom the truth that Jesus is the Son of God was as basic as the truth that the ground freezes in winter. They had five healthy sons—a bit boisterous in temperament, but good boys—and two daughters. Then, on Christmas Eve of 1927, Susie Emma brought forth a sixth son. Robert Joseph they named him, and he gave them yet another hope for an answer to that special request that they often brought before God. The Foxes did not have a great deal of exterior piety; their devotion, rather, was bound up with the practical realities of daily living and solidified by a basic and essential family spirituality. On occasion, however, Aloysius and Susie would ask God for a gift—that at least one of their six sons would become His priest.

Robert was still a baby when his father was called to God. He never knew his father by face, but he knew him by the tone that he had set in the family; an attitude that his mother would carry on, and that would pull the family through the difficult years that lay ahead. The whole family had to pitch in to keep the farm going during those times of the Great Depression, when nature herself seemed to have gone bankrupt and no rain fell from the sky. Somehow there was always food on the table, though not much of it. Clothes came from relatives in Minnesota, and heat came from the kitchen, rising up from a large wood stove. Winters were cold, and every day was long. Robert was already milking cows at the age of six, and as he got older he began to run the farm equipment. The family survived; in fact their poverty did not greatly hinder their happiness, for the home was laden with another kind of wealth.

"Blessed are the poor in spirit, for theirs is the kingdom of heaven" (Mt. 5:3). Every Sunday the Fox family would make the five mile trip into Watertown for Mass. Fr. O'Meara, the pastor, offered the Eucharist with a faith and sincerity that left a deep impression on Robert. Everyone in the area, it seemed, was Catholic—and many of them were related. Most of Robert's playmates were his first cousins and religion was a regular topic of conversation between families, and a source of unity. Robert had a sense, from a very early age, that a Catholic—wherever he might come from—was someone he could trust; someone who shared his beliefs and values, who had the peace of the same God in his heart. All Catholics are united in some very special way, the boy thought.

Before Robert had his first day of school, his mother took him aside and asked him, "What do you want to be when you grow up?" "Nothing," the little boy answered. "I thought you might like to be another Fr. O'Meara," suggested his mother, recalling her constant prayer for her sons. A sudden vision burst forth in the child's mind: How tremendous it would be to be a priest!

This thought remained with him through the years at Immaculate Conception school. His teachers were Franciscan nuns, and their manner and attitude—as well as what they taught—spoke to him of the power of humility. In fifth grade, one of the nuns taught him that the Mass is the Sacrifice of the Cross. Not understanding the theology, Robert thought that Jesus was suffering pain every time a Mass was said. But he loved Him all the more. Sometimes Robert would roll up a towel and wrap it around his neck like a roman collar in order to see what he would look like as a priest. Then there were pictures of Padre Pio; the boy marvelled at the power of Christ's priesthood, marked by the wounds that Padre Pio suffered in union with Jesus. The Eucharist began to be a vivid reality in Robert's experience; he would peek into the church in Watertown and draw near to the real presence of the Lord Jesus in the Blessed Sacrament—a Jesus who seemed to be calling, beckoning. . . .

High school, however, soon approached and brought with it the inevitable discovery of girls. Robert found that girls were really quite nice, and he rather enjoyed going to dances. He thought that perhaps he'd like to get married and have a family; he very much wanted a family, and besides—he'd have sons who could be priests, lots of sons. But then there was that special bond that draws all Catholics together—like a family. How he longed to embrace them all in Jesus. Would a family of 6 or 8 children be enough? No, he wanted thousands!

There was a tugging on his heart that would not go away, a fire that was the Holy Spirit reaching within him and casting his longings far beyond the high school, the girls, the dances, everything that fell short of Jesus. *"Yes, Lord, you know that I love you"* (John 23:16). The desire to be a priest, born of his parents' prayers, had taken firm hold in his heart and it would not be uprooted. *"Is not this the carpenter's son?"* (Mt. 26:55). Robert, however, faced another difficulty. It was quite uncommon for South Dakota farmboys to become priests; the pattern of life was fixed, and priests and nuns seemed to drop out of the sky rather than come off the farm. How would he tell his family of this seemingly strange ambition? A sudden fear took hold of him—would they take him seriously? Would they understand what he wanted? and why? Robert needed courage, or perhaps he would never leave the farm.

An accident with a hay rake, which broke his leg and even threatened his life, took him away from his farm duties for several months during his senior year of high school. This gave him time; time for prayer and reflection, time to develop courage. Robert Fox, internationally known leader in the apostolate, a light with the vigor of the earliest disciples—the clarity of St. Philip, the zeal of St. Steven, the dedication of St. Barnabas—began like them as a man afraid; even more so because his fear was of something undefinable; it was the fear of being misunderstood.

But the Spirit of the Lord lifted him up and his heart was filled with fortitude. Robert decided to tell a married sister, and rely on her to tell the rest of the family. The revelation of his desire came as a joy to the whole family, but especially to his mother whose special request, unknown to Robert, was now going to be fulfilled.

St. John's University in Collegeville, Minnesota was a center of liturgical development during the late 40's. The atmosphere gave the sense of a worldwide Church, and young Robert, who knew mostly plows, potato fields, and the parish church at Watertown, was a bit bewildered at first. The studies were formidable, and at first Robert feared that he would be overwhelmed. He prayed that God and the Blessed Mother might take special charge of his vocation, because he felt so powerless to do it alone.

"Take courage; it is I, do not be afraid" (Mt. 14:27). From that point on his grades improved, and he began to understand the depth of the Mystery that had called out to him from the tabernacle years ago. Among the most beautiful of doctrines that he explored was that of the Mystical Body of Christ—the Church as the extension of the Incarnation. Here was the source of that powerful union that he had always sensed among Catholics—their union as members of Christ Jesus; *"the unity of the Spirit in the bond of peace: one body and one Spirit . . . one God and Father of all, who is above all, and throughout all, and in us all"* (Eph. 4:3-6).

After two years at St. John's, Robert advanced to St. Paul's Seminary to conclude his studies. Here he lived an intense and structured prayer life, the form of which he has maintained to this day. At the seminary he learned to approach his priestly duties prayerfully, and how to reflect in those duties the Priesthood of Christ. Also, he was moved with the desire to preach the Word of God. During those days the seminarians would gather around a television set—a new piece of technology in 1953—and watch as Fulton Sheen grabbed hold of a fresh medium and claimed it for Christ. Robert was seized by the zeal that seemed to leap out of the television screen when Bishop Sheen spoke. "I thirst; I thirst for souls!" said the bishop. Robert felt this thirst, and longed to quench it by proclaiming the Gospel.

Finally ordination came on April 24, 1955. Robert felt as though the very statues in the Cathedral would come alive and cry out, "this man is unworthy!" His unworthiness, however, gave him a greater sense of the power of a God who *"can raise up children of Abraham from these very stones"* (Mt. 3:9). Stone though he might be, when the bishop of Sioux Falls laid hands on him, he was sealed with the mark of the High Priest, who *"because he continues forever, has an everlasting priesthood"* (Heb.

7:24). After the ordination, the priests' families approached the altar rail for a personal blessing. Susie Emma Fox shed a tear as she approached her son; a tear in memory of her husband's prayer—and hers—now answered to the Glory of God.

For young Fr. Fox, the priesthood meant the culmination of his devotion to the Mystical Body of Christ. He was filled with awe and wonder at each Mass he said; the richness of the presence of Christ and the intimacy of the union of the Mystical Body that was expressed in the liturgy increased his desire to "live the Mass" entirely in his priestly life—to be a victim, always pouring himself out in service to the members of Christ. Very early on, the basic approaches of Fr. Fox's pastoral life were established. This life centered on preaching, which produces the faith that makes incorporation into Christ possible and more vital. As a priest, Fr. Fox soon saw that all of his actions—indeed everything about himself—had a teaching significance. Mindful of this, he never failed to appear in clerical dress, because his mere identity spoke to people: "this man represents Jesus Christ."

From the beginning, Fr. Fox saw his preaching duties as particularly addressed to children. As an assistant in several rural parishes in South Dakota, he taught catechism right through the high school level. Here he saw the strength and significance of the basics of the faith, and how important they were to catechetical instruction. The rural people—modest, reserved, possessed of a natural humility—opened like blossoms when the young priest spoke of faith and devotion, and within these parishes he was already finding the "family" he had always desired.

Moreover it was his dedication to preaching that brought about the quite accidental series of events that launched Fr. Fox into his writing apostolate. During the early 1960's, after Fr. Fox had become pastor in Bristol, S.D., the *National Catholic Register* sent a letter to parish priests all across the country asking them not to neglect the preaching of sermons during the summer. Fr.

Fox wrote a letter to the editor of the *Register* in which he supported the *Register's* view and expounded at some length his own defense of the importance of preaching the Word of God at Mass. This was something central to his ministry, so the ideas flowed quite easily onto paper, and Fr. Fox sent the letter off without any difficulty. He was astonished when he received a reply praising his ideas, and suggesting that he write an article for *The Priest*, a magazine for clergy.

Fr. Fox didn't see himself as a writer, especially one who could be published in a national magazine. He was, after all, a pastor from the farmland of South Dakota—journalism was the furthest thing from his mind, and he didn't think that others would have too much interest in what he had to say. Therefore the idea of writing for *The Priest* was quickly forgotten.

Several months later, Fr. Fox was leafing through the latest issue of *The Priest*, and he came across an article written anonymously; this was not uncommon in the magazine which listed such articles under the pseudonym of "Sacerdos." This particular article was about sermons. As Fr. Fox read, he was struck by the fact that "Sacerdos" thought very much like himself about the need for consistent and fruitful preaching. He read on enthusiastically. Suddenly his mouth dropped open. "This *is* me," he gasped, recognizing the words and structure to be the very same as the letter he had written to the *Register*. The editor, perhaps suspecting Fr. Fox's own reluctance, had submitted the letter as an anonymous article to *The Priest*.

Fr. Fox was greatly encouraged by this unintentional success. Perhaps there was a way for him to serve God in the printed medium; at least he saw that it was possible for his writing to be published. So he began writing articles, and soon he found that his work was in great demand. Articles began to appear frequently in *Our Sunday Visitor*, *Homiletic and Pastoral Review*, and the *Register*, where Fr. Fox eventually secured a weekly column.

Fr. Fox viewed writing as a "prolongation and extension" of his preaching task, directed to those whom he could not reach personally. Meanwhile his primary focus continued to be personal contact in parish life. While he was busy attending to the needs of his parish community in Bristol, his bishop was participating in the sessions of the Second Vatican Council. Shortly after the promulgation of the Decree on Ecumenism, Fr. Fox—with the authorization of his bishop—conducted an ecumenical Advent prayer service along with three Protestant denominations. The service was attended by over six hundred people, and Bristol gained national attention with some observers calling the young and enthusiastic pastor a "new breed" priest.

Fr. Fox, however, was conscious that God is "ever Ancient, ever New," and with a sense of tradition and continuity he set out to perform the work of Vatican II. The Council revitalized his own commitment to catechesis, and he went about with even greater zeal in teaching the faith to God's smallest children. *"Let the little ones come to me"* (Lk. 18:18). At the same time Fr. Fox became keenly aware of difficulties arising in modern catechetics; people who claimed to be responding to the mandate of the council were actually watering down Catholic doctrine in the interests of some false sense of ecumenism or the dubious applications of certain fashionable trends in child psychology.

Fr. Fox's observance of these difficulties led to a book: *Religious Education; Its Effects, Its Challenges Today.* As the 1960's wore on, the atmosphere in catechetics became increasingly confused, and Fr. Fox's book was greeted enthusiastically by many as an answer to the rising problems, a light in the fog. Others, however, were determined to resist his efforts. As pastor in Milbank he sought to implement his vision of catechetics in the Catholic school. The principal and the school board opposed him, and tension gripped the entire parish. *"I come to bring not peace, but the sword"* (Mt. 10:34). Fr. Fox found that his commitment was being put to the test. Always desiring the welfare of his parish first, he now found himself the center of a controversy that was cutting a deep wound in his community. Perhaps it was his fault—perhaps he needed more patience in the situation? Or was he pushing his own view too far? Fr. Fox felt the sword within his own heart, driving him to seek a closer union with the suffering heart of Jesus. He wanted to know that he was doing God's will, so he asked for a sign relating to his life as a priest and catechist: "Is my work pleasing to you, O God?" The answer came through the Church: a few days before Christmas, Fr. Fox received a letter from Cardinal Wright, then secretary of the Congregation for the Clergy. "Keep writing, you are needed in America," the letter proclaimed as Cardinal Wright requested six copies of Fr. Fox's book. By the grace of God, Fr. Fox had found new confidence and courage—he stood with the Church.

In the midst of the crisis in the Church, Fr. Fox found his faith growing stronger. Important aspects of the priesthood were being called into question in the public forum, and Fr. Fox met these challenges in his preaching and in the deepening of interior life and commitment that resulted from it. The response to criticism of the priestly life—particularly celibacy—required a greater understanding of who the priest is and the nature of his ministry. Fr. Fox was drawn to reflect more and more on celibacy, the priesthood, and the Mystical Body in order to appreciate the Church and his own role in the troubled times following Vatican II.

"Blessed are they who hear the Word of God and keep it" (Lk. 11:28). In Fr. Fox's reflection, the Holy Spirit drew him toward the answer to today's crisis of faith. Modern man has forgotten how to believe; how to go beyond himself and find his true identity in the richness of God whom he is called to glorify in a unique fashion. All throughout his priestly life, Fr. Fox had dedicated himself to showing people how to live in faith. From his own work he realized the profound need for a model of the

Christian life; the response to God lived perfectly, full of power and love.

Since his childhood, Fr. Fox had always had a generous devotion to the Blessed Virgin Mary. Knowing that Mary brings her Son to all men and all men to her Son because of her unique and preeminent role in the salvation of the world, Fr. Fox had totally consecrated his priesthood to her at his ordination, so that he might be an instrument of her fundamental mission. When Mary was proclaimed Mother of the Church at the Second Vatican Council, Fr. Fox saw her role as source of that mystical Christian unity that is the Body of Christ her Son. Now, as faith was becoming more difficult and the minds of so many were becoming troubled and confused, Fr. Fox was drawn to Mary not only as the means—the mystery of her divine maternity—but also as the model of Christian perfection. Mary is the Woman of Faith; she is the Gospel lived in all its fullness, and union with her means a complete dedication to that Gospel. Living totally in the presence of God, and sharing and expressing in a unique way the fullness of God's life and love, Mary's identity is intimately linked with the personal vocation of each and every human being.

Fr. Fox sought a deeper and more formative union with the Mother of God, one that would infuse every detail of his ministry and priestly life. When the Pilgrim Virgin of Fatima statue came to the diocese of Sioux Falls in 1974, Fr. Fox decided to go to Fatima himself in order to find God's—and Mary's—will for him.

The message of Fatima meant above all devotion to the Immaculate Heart of Mary, embodying the fullness of Mary's response to God, and channelling Christ's life to each of the faithful. As he knelt in the chapel of the Apparitions at Cova da Iria, he asked Mary "what do you want of me?" There was no dramatic answer, no brilliant manifestation, no sudden flash of clarity. The prayer, however, took root as a new attitude within him. As the days wore on, an answer impressed itself upon his mind—consistent with all of his past work, yet representing a definite enrichment, a greater awareness: "Teach the fullness of Catholic faith to young people everywhere possible using Fatima as a vehicle."

"And from that hour the disciple took her into his home" (John 19:27). Fr. Fox returned to South Dakota with renewed zeal, and became involved with the World Apostolate of Fatima. He produced a tape series—*To Teach as Mary Did at Fatima*—as an immediate application of his commitment to preach the Gospel through the Fatima message of conversion, penance, and the love of God.

Then, as chairman of a Fatima Youth Seminar in Detroit, Fr. Fox introduced his ideas for making outreach to young people a vital part of the Fatima apostolate. He founded a youth division of the World Apostolate of Fatima, and wrote *Catholic Truth for Youth*. At this time, however, the specifics of the task with youth remained undefined—how could he preach the Gospel anew to young people by means of the message of Fatima?

"Did I not promise that you would see the glory of God displayed?" (Jn. 11:40). While leading a group of adults in a Holy Year Pilgrimage through Fatima to Rome in 1975, Fr. Fox had an inspiration: What better way to bring the Fatima message to young people than by bringing young people to Fatima! A Youth Pilgrimage, run like a retreat, would provide an opportunity for young people to meet the Lord Jesus through the conversion of heart called for by Fatima and the Gospel it reflects. This inspiration was the beginning of the Youth for Fatima Pilgrimages which Fr. Fox has led each year since 1975. To this day the youth pilgrimages—one for boys and one for girls aged 15-22—are the high point of Fr. Fox's year, filled with tremendous spiritual fruits. On these trips many young people come to grips for the first time with the sins that this difficult age so strongly encourages, and these young people—filled with a newfound hope in the merciful and transforming love of

Christ—approach the Sacrament of Reconciliation in great numbers. Fr. Fox recalls how some young people—touched by the Holy Spirit and delivered from so much unhappiness and confusion—will proclaim with tears in their eyes, "Thank God a priest finally told me the truth about my sins." This truth, which because of its difficulty is so often neglected, can only be presented with the ever-present invitation to God's mercy, and the result is a transformation of heart which for so many young people is the first step to their own interior union with the Immaculate Heart of Mary, the perfect Christian life.

During the most recent pilgrimages in the Summer of 1986, the Bishop of Leiria-Fatima, Alberto Cosme do Amaral, greeted the young people at the Cova da Iria—the site of the apparitions—and said: "You are an example to the youth of Portugal. You are an example to the youth of the whole world. Because Fatima is difficult, it is especially for youth." Bishop Amaral also blessed a replica of the statue of Our Lady at Fatima for Fr. Fox, announcing, "Wherever this statue is, there the message of Fatima will be." Thus, Fr. Fox sees the youth pilgrimages as a particular expression of his vocation as a catechist and minister of God's Word and the highlight of his own call to serve God among "the little children."

It was during that same Holy Year tour in 1975 that Fr. Fox met a man who was to have an important influence on his more recent activities. Gino Burresi of the Oblates of the Virgin Mary—possessor of the miraculous charism of the stigmata (the wounds of Christ)—greeted Fr. Fox and some of his pilgrims at San Vittorino, Italy. The two men found a deep spiritual rapport. Fr. Fox visited then-Brother Gino several times over the next few years. He was inspired by Br. Gino's intensity of life, his singular dedication to the Gospel, and the dramatic physical character of his witness of suffering. As this inspiration developed, Fr. Fox conceived the notion of writing a book on Br. Gino's life in order to communicate his witness and charism to a wider audience. *Call of Heaven*, now in its second edition (which includes the ordination of Gino Burresi to the priest-hood), has strengthened the faith of many who have read it, and has drawn some of these into the religious life.

The book on Fr. Gino, as well as the constant work with youth, brought about for Fr. Fox an increasing involvement with vocations. Many young men looked up to him as a strong defender of truth as well as a man of evangelical compassion and zeal. His preaching and writing had placed the desire for the priesthood within the hearts of many of these young men, who often sought him out for guidance.

"Do not think that it is you who have chosen me, rather it is I who have chosen you" (Jn. 15:16). Directing the vocations of young men became an increasingly prominent feature of Fr. Fox's work. This prompted him to found a priestly formation program with a specific orientation to the apostolate of the me-dia—the priesthood and the media were, after all, the two areas most familiar to him. He called his program the Sons of the Immaculate Heart. In the fall of 1982 with the encouragement of his bishop and a personal expression of support from Cardi-nal Pironio, head of the Congregation for Religious, Fr. Fox be-gan his program, and soon he had seven candidates living with him at his parish in Redfield, S.D.

At this time all the "signs" indicated that the Sons of the Immaculate Heart would be a great success, and inquiries and support poured in from all across the country. During this time Fr. Fox also produced a video cassette catechism course, *Sharing the Faith* ("Instructions in the Catholic Faith"), in which he re-vived the style and potential of Catholic television preaching. In addition he maintained parish work, consistent writing, and the Fatima pilgrimages. His work schedule reflected a rich harvest, but perhaps too rich for one man. In time the demands on his energy began to take their toll, and his health began to decline.

"Blessed are the sorrowful, they shall be consoled" (Mt. 5:4). Fr. Fox trusted that God would not allow his own limitations to hinder the ministry of salvation that was entrusted to him. But

he did not realize that now—when it seemed that his active apostolate was so necessary—God was calling him instead to a ministry of suffering. His health suddenly collapsed; at Fatima he was struck with pneumonia so severe that he lost the pattern of his voice, the very tool with which he had brought God's word to so many. The bishop ordered the Sons of the Immaculate Heart to disband; Fr. Fox had to retreat to a rural environment, regain his strength, and learn to speak all over again.

Rendered dumb and helpless by the mystery of God's providence, Fr. Fox entered into the immense darkness and smallness of "thy will be done." He experienced a new dimension of conformity to the Immaculate Heart of Mary, one that goes beyond particular plans and ambitions—even holy ambitions—and embraces the "fiat" simply for the sake of "magnifying the Lord." Fr. Fox did not understand why God had taken away his strength, or why the Sons had failed. He only knew that this was what God wanted, and that his very helplessness was now a vehicle for God's glory.

"For he has regarded the lowliness of his handmaid" (Lk. 1:48). In time Fr. Fox grew well and regained his speech. He wrote a new book, *Immaculate Heart of Mary; True Devotion,* in which he enriches the spirituality of St. Louis de Montfort by casting it in the context of devotion to the Immaculate Heart, a devotion that has become the very core and substance of his own life. In 1985 he came to St. Mary of Mercy parish in Alexandria, where he is building a shrine to Our Lady of Fatima in a spot that is very near to the center of the North American continent. Here Fr. Fox will host the first Marian Congress in America in September of 1987. The Bishop of Leiria-Fatima will visit the United States for the first time to attend the Congress and dedicate the new shrine. He will also crown the replica statue with a crown like that on the original statue at Fatima.

Fr. Fox will also launch a new quarterly magazine in January of 1986. Called *Youth for Fatima,* the new publication is in-

tended primarily for young people between the ages of 16 and
25, and will use the Fatima message to inspire its readers with
greater devotion to the Church and renewed zeal for her mission in the world. *Youth for Fatima* will be published by Trinity
Communications at $6.00 per year. Meanwhile Fr. Fox continues
his writing, preaching, and spiritual guidance to youth all over
the country. And, as always, he remains dedicated to his parish,
especially the children, all of whom he continues to teach just as
he has in every parish he has ever served.

   *"What you have hidden from the learned and the clever you
have revealed to merest children"* (Lk. 10:21). Fr. Robert J. Fox
"knows the Father" because he enters with childlike simplicity
into the mystery of the Trinity. In 1979, Pope John Paul II
spoke with Fr. Fox, and encouraged him to pattern his life after
the Sermon on the Mount. The Pope's advice points to the message of the Kingdom of God, fully revealed as the Mystical
Body of Christ and lived in union with the Immaculate Heart
of Mary, Mother of that Body, source of the deep and personal
union of all its members, and of the members to the Head. This
message of unity has been the strength and essence of Fr. Fox's
priesthood, its motivation and driving force. With and through
Mary, he is present to the Person of Jesus Christ and receives a
share in the work of building the Kingdom. In this way Fr. Fox
stands as an instrument of God's power, drawing those he encounters into the unity of love that God wills for all men; that
unity which is Jesus Christ—the Christ that his soul proclaims,
the Christ in whom he rejoices.

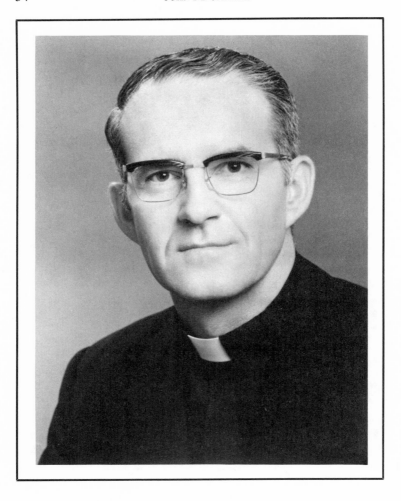

II.
Father Kenneth Baker, S.J.

Priests are called to proclaim the saving truth of Jesus Christ in a direct manner, as his witnesses. For many priests in the United States today, the Gospel witness is a lonely one; not only has secular America become hostile to the Christian message, but also affairs of the Church in various parts of the country have fallen under the control of men who lack vision, a sense of the unity and universality of the Church, or even fidelity. In these places the faithful minister of Jesus Christ must often face a kind of psychological persecution: a relegation to an insignificant role in the life of his local church, and criticism—veiled or open—for being somehow "outdated" because of his loyalty to the teachings of the Church, as if the fullness of the Gospel had gone out of season.

"I will not leave you desolate; I will come to you" (Jn. 14:18). These priests have a great need for solidarity, consolation, and accurate information on the state of the Church in America and all over the world. They need a link to foster communication, stimulate legitimate opinion, and aid in the discernment of spirits that is so necessary to the present situation. For such purposes, modern media present a unique opportunity, and one magazine in particular has taken the lead in strengthening the bonds among priests, speaking to all those who are truly con-

cerned about the Church of God. One can almost hear a chorus of priests sighing with joy and relief each month as they remove from the mailboxes the latest issue of *Homiletic and Pastoral Review*, realizing that they are not alone.

Engaged full-time in this task of fostering priestly solidarity is a man who has seen many aspects of the priestly vocation—and many of its trials—in his own life. Father Kenneth Baker, S.J. brings a wealth of understanding—born of the Holy Spirit and experience—to his work as editor-in-chief of one of the most important magazines for priests in the English speaking world, infusing his efforts with the particular spirit that characterizes the Society of Jesus and has carried him through the whole of his priestly life: the habit of being a joyful and brave soldier of Christ. *"For thy steadfast love is before my eyes, and I walk in faithfulness to thee"* (Ps. 26:3).

The joy Fr. Baker brings to his brother priests, however, was a scarce commodity in Tacoma, Washington in November 1929, less than a month after the infamous Stock Market crash initiated the Great Depression that would paralyze America for a decade. Kenneth Sr. and Catherine Baker had been young and carefree in 1929, both working at well-paying jobs. By the time little Ken was born on November 12, however, they were greatly distressed about the future. Before a year had passed his parents divorced, and the baby was given to his maternal grandparents—Daniel and Mary Browne—to be raised. From that time on Ken would have little contact with his parents, and his home life centered on the Browne family where the two youngest children, an uncle and an aunt, still lived. Daniel Browne was a construction foreman and a dockworker, a burly man who had worked his way across the country from Nova Scotia, and still had a touch of the pioneer spirit that was rapidly disappearing from the west. When he had arrived in Spokane at the turn of the century it was little more than an outpost at the end of the frontier. In 1920 he moved his family to Tacoma, an infant port on the Puget Sound looking out toward the Pacific. Commerce with the Orient, however, enabled Tacoma to grow rapidly into an important center for shipping, and the Tacoma of Ken Baker's youth was a regular city with some of the color and a touch of the decadence that grows up around centers of trade.

Because of the confusing circumstances of his earliest years, young Ken had never been baptized. His father and his grandfather were not Catholic, and no one had ever brought him to the local church. The time had come, however, for him to go to school, and his grandmother—who was a practicing Catholic—decided that Ken should go to the school of St. Leo's parish, despite the fact that the parochial school was more expensive and less convenient than the local public school. So at the age of five Ken Baker was baptized into the death and resurrection of Jesus Christ; at the time the boy thought very little of it, seeing it as just another part of starting school.

"Make me to know thy ways, O Lord, teach me thy paths" (Ps. 25:4). In retrospect, however, Fr. Baker sees the decision to go to Catholic school as a pivotal one in his life; not only did it provide the occasion for his baptism, it also provided the kind of environment in which his life in Christ could grow and flourish. The Franciscan Sisters who staffed St. Leo's had a dedication to the children and to their consecrated life that impressed Ken very deeply. It was the life of the sisters as a "witness to the transcendence of God" that was most instructive to Ken and gave him a depth of faith; nevertheless he showed no signs in his early school days that he would one day devote himself to the service of God. Ken was a normal boy, getting in and out of various kinds of trouble like other boys his age. "When I did wrong, though, I knew it," he remembers, reflecting on the kindness in confession that Fr. Augustine Krebsbach, the round and jolly Jesuit pastor of St. Leo's, always showed toward the children of the parish. Vocation, however, was the furthest thing from his mind at that time. Once in religion class, the sister asked the boys how many of them thought they might like

to be priests. Every boy in the class raised his hand except one;
Ken Baker sat at his desk, arms at his sides—he could not
imagine himself ever being a priest.

When it came time for Ken to go to high school, he faced
another important decision. The family was very poor; his
grandfather had suffered a stroke and could no longer work.
Grandmother supported the whole family earning $6.00 a week
as a restaurant cook. Ken had hoped to go to Bellarmine High
School but he knew he could never afford the $80.00 yearly tu-
ition, a significant sum of money in those days. So Ken prepared
to enroll in the public high school.

Here Ken faced another significant moment in his life, and
an opportunity opened for him through the generosity of an
uncle, who offered to pay the first year of Ken's tuition at Bellarmine, and to employ him so he could pay the rest of the tuition himself. Ken's uncle owned a restaurant—a diner with
counters, booths, pinball machines, and fifty cent luncheon spe-
cials. For the next four years, Ken attended Bellarmine High
School and worked afternoons and weekends at the diner, first
as a dishwasher and then as a fry cook. During this time Ken
grew to maturity, and his world was shaped by two major factors—the busy, varied, worldly life that continually poured
through the diner, and the peace and power of the Jesuit life
that formed the spirit of his school.

The restaurant work gave Ken the chance to become fi-
nancially independent. At age sixteen he bought a car—a 1938
Dodge four door sedan. He was glad that his grandparents did
not have to strain their own budget to support him, and his
independence gave him a certain self-confidence and knowledge
of the ways of the world. A good deal of that world passed
through the diner while Ken flipped hamburgers at the grill behind the counter. The war was on, and three branches of the
service had bases in Tacoma; this meant that the diner was always full of soldiers and sailors, bringing with them their ap-
petites and their desire for a "good time." Also, some of the

waitresses were prostitutes who used their job as a contact point for male customers. Everyone knew Ken—the grill was out in the open, and he could see everything that went on in the restaurant. The young man was well-liked, but he was struck by a sense of futility and lack of commitment that seemed to dominate the lives of so many people. His Aunt and Uncle were outstanding people, but their customers were as varied as the world itself; thus by the time he was a senior in high school Ken had learned many things about the secular world, and he had no illusions about its promises. *"For they are a nation void of counsel, and there is no understanding in them"* (Deut. 32:28).

Meanwhile Bellarmine was the center of a healthy and active adolescent life. At first Ken did not devote much time to his studies; he was caught up in the new-found excitement of social life—dances, parties, and girls. There were two Catholic girls' schools nearby, and Ken went on many dates, usually consisting of a movie and then rootbeer and hamburgers.

As a junior, however, Ken began to pay more attention to school; the thought occurred to him that he might like to go to college, something that no one in the family had ever done. He even thought about joining the navy and becoming a pilot. With these things in mind, Ken became a dedicated and successful student. And with this increase in his sense of responsibility came an increase in faith. During Lent of his junior year Ken decided to go to Mass every day; for the first time in his life he was going beyond the requirements of his faith—it was a glimpse of a call to draw more deeply into the mystery of Jesus.

Meanwhile Ken strove to become a leader among his peers. He ran for student body president and developed a sophisticated campaign. He had a friend who flew airplanes, and he paid him five dollars to drop five hundred "vote for Baker" fliers over the school. Unfortunately a steady wind blew the fliers away from the school grounds and scattered them all over the football field. The principal was not pleased and Ken found

himself spending an afternoon picking fliers off the field. He
lost the election.

Nevertheless Ken had plunged into the spirit of his school
and was involved in many activities. Then, as a senior, he began
keeping regular company with a cheerleader from one of the
rival schools. As Ken Baker approached high school graduation
he had a steady income, a car, and a girlfriend. It did not appear
as though there was any room in the picture for the consideration of the priesthood.

But something was happening inside Ken. His high school
life had introduced him to the reality of the charism of the Society of Jesus. Most of the high school teachers were Jesuit
scholastics, men only a few years older than the students. Nevertheless these men were professed members of the Jesuit community and were preparing themselves for priesthood. There
was a joy in their work, a purpose and direction that was a
sharp contrast to the world of the diner. These men had discovered something—a sense of dedication, happiness, and service—that was shaping their entire lives, and this sense—this
discovery—infused the spirit of Bellarmine High School. In this
way it gradually touched Ken's heart, beginning with subtlety
like an acorn and growing slow and steady like an oak.

"Awake, awake, put on your strength, O Zion" (Is. 52:1). In
the spring of his senior year, the buds appeared. The chaplain at
Bellarmine suggested to Ken that he might like to try the novitiate of the Society of Jesus. The suggestion took Ken by sur-
prise, but the more he thought about it, the more he realized
that the novitiate would give him the opportunity to discover
the reality that lay behind the commitment that had so greatly
impressed him—the foundation of the joyfulness that made the
Jesuits so unique.

At this time Ken did not have any profound awareness of
a priestly vocation. He only knew that he wanted to try the Jesuit life; there was something about it that seemed to embody
all the things he hoped to be in his own life. His girlfriend Pat,

needless to say, was not greatly pleased with Ken's new plans, but she respected and supported his decision. Thus on August 15, 1947, Ken began two years of "courtship" as a Jesuit novice.

This was the time during which a young man would steep himself in the way of the Society, and the Society would carefully investigate its candidate. It was an intense life in a monastic framework, filled with a constant and regular regimen of prayer, work, and instruction—and, most importantly, learning the demands of obedience. *"Blessed are all who take refuge in Him"* (Ps. 1:11).

As the novitiate progressed, Ken found that his interest in the Jesuits had blossomed into love, and after two years he was ready to commit himself to the Society of Jesus, embracing all of its rigors and hoping for its rewards. On the feast of the Assumption 1949, Kenneth Baker took his perpetual vows. As he remembers it, "You commit yourself to the Society but the Society does not commit itself to you." A great deal of preparation lay ahead, but Ken was determined to persevere for as long as the Society of Jesus saw fit.

In any case the priesthood was still eleven years away. As the Jesuit system progressed, structured discipline became more relaxed and the candidate was expected to maintain the spiritual and intellectual life on his own motivation. First, there were two years of classical study, followed by three years of philosophy. Here Ken was able to develop more personal friendships, play a great deal of sports (which are always a major part of Jesuit recreation), and enjoy intellectual opportunities that gave him a lasting love for learning.

At the end of philosophical study, Ken became a scholastic, and was assigned to teach Latin and Greek at Gonzaga Preparatory School in Spokane. During these years Ken developed an ability and a liking for teaching. It appeared as though he would be making his mark behind the desk of a classroom.

With this in mind, the Provincial asked Ken if he wanted to go to Europe for theological study. Ken was excited about the prospect of studying with the Jesuit faculty at the University of Innsbruck, although at the time his academic major was Classics.

Within a year at Innsbruck, however, the excitement and challenge of theology had set him aflame. Ken realized that theology—with its capacity to deepen the whole perspective of faith—was where his future lay. The enthusiasm of the Innsbruck faculty combined with the unique atmosphere of the Austrian highlands made a deep impression. Ken became fluent in German, comfortable in getting around Europe, an expert skier, and a student with great interest and concern about theological matters in the Church. During this period he also became a sharer in the priesthood of Jesus Christ.

"My shield is with God, who saves the upright in heart" (Ps. 7:10). On July 26, 1960 Kenneth Baker was ordained at Holy Trinity Church in Innsbruck. He was a priest forever, in the soldierly spirit of St. Ignatius, the evangelical spirit of St. Francis Xavier, the intellectual spirit of St. Robert Bellarmine: a tradition of warriors for Christ, whose swords were justice, discernment and love. The Jesuits were trained to fight to the death, but their enemies were sin, ignorance, and error, and they strived continually to bring opponents of the Gospel to death in Christ Jesus—the "death" of conversion—so that they might rise again as friends and fellow soldiers.

For thirteen years the Society of Jesus had been fashioning a sword for Kenneth Baker: its hilt was a keen mind, its blade a disciplined application of skill sharpened by the sacramental powers of priesthood, and its scabbard a peaceful heart born of continual interior communication with Christ. It was a sword that would carry him through the significant and often perilous years that lay ahead.

After his final year of theology in 1961, Fr. Baker received the Licenciate degree and headed home. The last year of Jesuit training is the tertianship, a kind of "novitiate" into the world of preaching the Gospel, where the young priest prepares himself spiritually and exercises his priesthood in a variety of pastoral situations. Fr. Baker prepared to do his tertianship in his home state of Washington, but upon his return he found himself bound for a teaching position at Gonzaga University. The philosophy department desperately needed another teacher, so the Provincial asked Fr. Baker to postpone his tertianship and fill in temporarily. Fr. Baker lectured for two years on logic, philosophy of man, and philosophy of God. After his long awaited tertianship in 1963, Fr. Baker looked over his theological background and decided that he needed more familiarity with Sacred Scripture. With this in mind he asked to pursue his graduate degree in Marquette University's religious studies program. He received his Ph.D. in 1967, and returned to Gonzaga University to join the theological faculty as an assistant professor.

During this time Fr. Baker became aware of a sudden and swift current of innovation that seemed to seize hold of the universities and the priests and nuns who staffed them. Gonzaga was different when he returned in the fall of 1967. Nuns were beginning to remove their habits and lose their religious identity. Priests, seminarians, and nuns would gather for "beer parties" on the campus. Fr. Baker attended a few of these parties out of a desire to see and understand what was going on, and he quickly sensed an unhealthy spirit, a breakdown in the commitment to a complete and exclusive following of Christ, a haze dimming the witness to the reality of eternal life. *"For this people's heart has grown dull, and their ears are heavy of hearing...."* (Mt. 13:15).

Fr. Baker knew that this spirit was a false one, and his response was to draw more closely to the spirit of the Church, the guidance that manifested the voice of the Holy Spirit. "Both arms around the Pope, that's my principle," Fr. Baker notes when reflecting on these times. With this principle firmly in mind, he became chairman of the theology department in 1968. In the summer of that year Pope Paul VI reaffirmed the Church's teaching on sexuality and its inseparable connection to life and love. Catholic university professors all over America rose in rebellion; Gonzaga's faculty, however, remained loyal and gave a series of lectures in support of *Humanae Vitae*. Fr. Baker preached it from the pulpit of the Jesuit Church in Spokane.

As he gained experience in both academics and administration, Fr. Baker began to develop a strong sense of what was needed to preserve and advance a truly apostolic character in Catholic education. *". . . be wise as serpents and innocent as doves"* (Mt. 10:16). He began publishing articles and delivering lectures on the topic, and his perspective—with its emphasis on bringing out the specifically Christian identity of Catholic educational institutions—began to attract attention. A sermon he preached on Catholic education at the opening Mass of the Jesuit University of Seattle was especially well received. In a period when many Catholic colleges were "secularizing" by turning over control of their institutions to lay boards of directors, Fr. Baker was defending the preservation of ecclesiastical affiliation, and he was instrumental in securing Jesuit control in the revised charter of Gonzaga.

". . . the Holy Spirit, whom the Father will send in my name, he will teach you all things . . ." (Jn. 14:25). Fr. Baker longed to imbue the institutions he served with that same Jesuit spirit of solidarity and service that had played such an important part in his years of school. And he was trying to accomplish this as a teacher and an administrator in the midst of one of the most stormy periods in the history of Catholic education—indeed of all education. But the strongest winds were yet to blow.

On Thanksgiving weekend of 1969, the Provincial called Fr. Baker into his office. He had made a decision: the president of Seattle University was to be replaced, and the Provincial had decided to appoint Fr. Baker. The news came as quite a shock to a man who had just celebrated his 40th birthday. In retrospect Fr. Baker wishes that he had had more experience in dealing with people before taking the job; at that time, however, neither he nor his superiors had anticipated the turmoil that was to come.

On February 1, 1970, Fr. Baker was installed as president of Seattle University. Within a few months the Kent State killings and the invasion of Cambodia touched off a wave of campus radicalism all across the country. Student riots plagued Seattle University all year; many of them—Fr. Baker was convinced—were manufactured by professional agitators. Revolutionary organizations threatened Fr. Baker's life, and for three weeks at one point he had 24-hour police protection. People broke into his office and smashed furniture. On two occasions mobs of students forced their way into Fr. Baker's office, holding him a virtual prisoner while they shouted their complaints and demands. The situation was desperate, but Fr. Baker saw no willingness to dialogue on the part of these student radicals; they were not even raising responsible issues or objections. He perceived that the agitation was designed to wreak havoc on the school, and his conclusion was that he must remain firm. *"Cleave to him and do not depart"* (Sir. 2:3).

The policy might have succeeded if all those involved in the university had supported it. Several benefactors and other influential people, however, favored a conciliatory approach, and began to press for Fr. Baker's resignation. *". . . no city or house divided against itself will stand"* (Mt. 12:25). Caught between radical student politics and divided perspectives on school policy, Fr. Baker realized that he would not be able to implement his vision of Catholic education—he could not even effectively govern the university. So, after nine rocky months as president, Fr. Baker resigned, greatly discouraged because it seemed as though he had failed. Failure was a new experience for Fr. Baker, yet it was the experience of the cross and in this respect it touched upon the central element of his priesthood, the deepest meaning of conformity to the Person of Christ. *"Thou hast been to me a fortress and a refuge in the day of my distress"* (Ps. 59:56). It is not surprising, then, that his "failure"—which had resulted from his own uncompromising adherence to principle and his conscientious assessment of the situation—touched off a series of events that would bring him to New York and the *Homiletic and Pastoral Review*.

"You shall see, and your heart shall rejoice" (Is. 66:14). In reality, Fr. Baker had only lost a battle. William Buckley admired his stand at Seattle and invited him to New York as a guest on "Firing Line." It was in New York in December of 1970, while at a restaurant with Fr. Baker and another Jesuit, that Fr. Daniel Lyons (laicized in 1976) unveiled an idea to buy the faltering and nearly bankrupt *Homiletic and Pastoral Review*, and Kenneth Baker—who was suddenly in need of a new assignment—seemed the perfect choice for Editor-in-Chief.

The whole plan was suddenly set in motion. Their Provincial gave his approval, and Lyons set up a company that bought the magazine on a three year payment plan. Fr. Baker returned to Washington, packed his bags and moved to New York. By April 1971 the first issue was ready, featuring a prominent editorial by the new editor: "Catholic and Proud of it." The principle that guided his academic work—indeed his whole life as a Christian—became operative in a new circumstance, a new task: "We came out four square in favor of the Pope and the magisterium."

"Faithfulness will spring from the ground, and righteousness will look down from the sky" (Ps. 85:11). Fr. Baker soon found that priests all over America were looking for a trustworthy voice, a voice that would echo the Holy Father and provide a focal point for unity and instruction. Almost immediately there were four thousand new subscribers, and letters poured in from priests in distress, so thankful to find a "beacon of light in a dark storm."

Thus for the last sixteen years *Homiletic and Pastoral Review* has been Fr. Baker's main occupation. Each day he must answer a large volume of mail, much of which involves questions about the teaching of the Church or other points of information regarding Catholic things. *". . . let us hold true to what we have attained"* (Phil. 3:16). As a magazine identifiably dedicated to the authentic teaching mission in the Church, *HPR* is a magnet for articles on almost all Church topics from a perspective loyal to the See of Peter. Unsolicited manuscripts arrive at a rate of one per day, and Fr. Baker reads, evaluates, and accepts or rejects each one promptly.

In addition, one of the most significant aspects of *HPR* is its series of homilies for every Sunday and Holy Day of the year. Fr. Baker solicits a cycle of homilies one year in advance from a variety of priests who are noted for their fidelity to the teaching of the Church. He hopes that these homilies will serve as a wellspring of ideas for priests as they prepare their Sunday sermons. Fr. Baker hopes in this way to reach a large percentage of Catholics who attend Sunday Mass, which is possible given the fact that *HPR* comes to nearly half the parishes in the United States.

Also, of the 14,000 subscriptions, 2200 go overseas to Rome, Africa, missionaries in Japan and India and other parts of Asia. Today the *HPR* reaches all of the English-speaking world, and has received the encouragement of more than one official in the Roman Curia.

"While you have the light, believe in the light, that you may become sons of light" (Jn. 12:36). The necessity and success of *HPR* convinced Fr. Baker of the need to branch out into other sectors of the media. In 1974 Fr. Lyons founded Catholic Views Broadcasts, Inc. When Lyons left the active ministry in 1975, Fr. Baker took over as Director. Every week since 1975 this company has produced a fifteen minute interview program called "Views of the News," which is syndicated to over 100 radio stations. The program features prominent Catholic commentators addressing timely issues, such as abortion, euthanasia, pornography, communism, and situations in foreign countries, from the perspective of Catholic social teaching.

The media work of Fr. Baker received the support of many important people in New York. Among them was Cardinal Paul Yu-Pin of Taiwan, who provided office space for the magazine and radio apostolates at his New York residence—86 Riverside Drive in Manhattan. Here Fr. Baker has added another area of expertise to his repertoire: Chinese cuisine. He and Fr. Paul Chan of the Chinese Catholic Information Center co-authored a booklet titled *How to Order a Real Chinese Meal* that takes the reader through a bit of history and geography as well as providing a road map for making the most of a menu in a Chinese restaurant.

After several years of producing an intellectually oriented magazine directed primarily toward priests, Fr. Baker decided to initiate a pocket-size, inspirational, lay-oriented magazine as well. Thus, in 1978, *Key to Happiness* was born. *Key* takes a positive tone, offering devotions, lives of the saints, prayer, and experiences of God's grace and healing. This small magazine has a subscription of 25,000, and when Fr. Baker goes on a lecture tour it is often the thing people immediately identify: "Oh that *Key*, I carry that with me wherever I go, I give it to my friends, I just love it."

When he is not supervising operation and production in his multi-faceted media apostolate, Fr. Baker attends important meetings of Church leaders—not only to report on a significant story, but also to get a sense of the pulse of the Church. Among the meetings he never misses are the annual bishop's meeting and the international Synods in Rome. More recently he has increased his involvement in the work of fostering spirituality, regularly giving retreats and leading European pilgrimages. He also provides spiritual direction and exhortation for three convents in the New York City area.

"Rejoice in the Lord always; again I will say, Rejoice. Let all men know your forebearance" (Phil. 4:4). All these activities make up the days and months in the life of Fr. Kenneth Baker, S.J. In each of them he is decidedly priest and Jesuit—this

means that he is a leader, and also a man who may be compelled to suffer because of the leadership he provides in response to the call of the Spirit. It is a leadership, however, whose effects are felt across America, giving form and direction to a wide section of the Church in the United States by manifesting the whole Church of Christ, united and universal. Fr. Baker succeeds in providing this leadership because he stays close to the Church, always seeking to discern her direction in the spirit of faithfulness to the Gospel. Loyal Jesuit that he is, Fr. Baker has seized hold of that Gospel and raised it in proclamation with courage and joy. This proclamation has a vitality that touches and enlivens those priests who rely on his work, drawing them ever more closely to Jesus, to the Jesus who says *"I am with you all days . . ."* (Mt. 28:20).

III.
Msgr. Richard J. Schuler

Incense rises from around the marble altar, drawing one's eyes from the Lamb of God at the front of the altar to the painting of Christ crucified above it, the Blessed Virgin and St. John standing at His feet. On the altar a priest is making present that all-encompassing sacrifice, *"the offering of the body of Jesus Christ once for all"* (Heb. 10:10). He invites the congregation to pray and they respond in a resounding tone that fills the church with the sound of that tongue which is the sign of the Universal Church; the Latin of the See of Peter, in which Christians of every race and nation give glory to the Father through Jesus Christ *"that they may be one, as We are One"* (Jn. 17:11).

A choir begins to chant, drawing all who hear into the mystery of God's salvation. The congregation is intensely aware of this reality, and involved in it as they offer themselves in union with the Eucharistic sacrifice. Here indeed is the People of God, *"a royal priesthood, a holy nation, a people set apart"* (1 Pt. 2:9). Every moment of the liturgy speaks of the offering "holy and undefiled" of Jesus Christ to the Father, the mystery of redemption filling every mind and heart, informing every action, every word, every strand of music.

Liturgical renewal is centered on Jesus Christ, and because of this it makes unique demands on those who share in His ministerial priesthood. Its essence is to involve the faithful more deeply in the liturgy; to strengthen the Mystical Body of Christ. Here at St. Agnes Church in St. Paul, Minnesota something extraordinary is happening—authentic liturgical renewal. There are many parishes where "renewal" has meant divorcing the liturgy from its past, or from the norms that give it unity and meaning. For St. Agnes, however, it has meant reflecting the Universal Church. This effort of renewal is led by Msgr. Richard Schuler, a man who has molded his priesthood according to the Church, always listening attentively to her voice; a man who stands with the Universal Church as she authentically presents herself today; a man who calls the Catholic Church—the Bride of Christ—the "great love of my life."

"The God who gives joy to my youth" (Ps. 43:4). It is not surprising that Richard Schuler's heart was drawn to the Church, for his young life was surrounded by evidence of her truth and splendor. He was born on December 30, 1920 across the river in Minneapolis, one of three children who survived for Otto and Wilhelmine Schuler. Theirs was a "very Catholic" neighborhood, dominated by Ascension Church and its school and convent. Young Richard was summoned to lunch and supper each day by the Angelus bell. The priests of the parish were dedicated and well loved, as were the sisters. Often, when one of the sisters needed transportation in her tasks, Otto Schuler would drive her, and the boy Richard would go along in the back, catching a glimpse of the motherhouse and wondering at all that it represented.

Catholicism was the root of a joyous home life, filled with the security, warmth, and love of an Austrian/Bavarian household. Discipline was enforced primarily through the integrity and strength of character of his parents. There were not many "rules" in the family, but the Schuler children were well aware of what their parents expected of them, and failure brought with it its own shame.

Richard's faith, then, was firm from childhood. The support of family and neighborhood reflected the general vitality of the Church in the Twin Cities as a whole. Richard was never made to feel that being a Catholic was unusual or somehow incompatible with social life. When he was old enough Richard began school at Ascension, and soon displayed an interest in music. At the age of eight he began studying piano with the sisters; and sometimes, like other children, he had to be prodded into his daily practice. Nevertheless he was soon contributing to the music of the liturgies in his parish.

As he grew older, Richard's appreciation for the Church grew deeper. He entered DeLaSalle High School and began to learn more about the Church's history, her great saints, her impact on culture, art, and—as always—music. The Pilgrim Church, in her journey through this life, touches upon many aspects of earthly experience and transforms them into signs of the hope that she has in the coming of the Kingdom. Richard saw this hope built into the institutions and the routines of his youth, but most profoundly in the splendor of the liturgy. One Easter Sunday Richard traveled with his father to St. Paul Cathedral to see a pontifical High Mass. He was captivated not simply by the form of expression, but also by its meaning. *"Oh death where is thy victory, oh death where is thy sting"* (1 Cor. 15:55)? Jesus Christ is God in the flesh whose death had brought life to the world, and everything about the Church proclaimed this reality.

Richard wished to become immersed in this proclamation. Reflecting on the enthusiasm of his high school years, he says, "The Church was everything that we were. It was our whole life." As Lent of his sophomore year approached, Richard made a resolution—to unite himself each day to Christ in the Eucharistic sacrifice. When he saw the richness of Christian life—its prayers and processions, its worship and witness; when he heard the Word of God, or the chant that raises the heart to God—when he saw and heard these things he saw and heard Jesus Christ. Now he wanted others, in seeing and hearing himself, to see and hear Christ.

"If you want to be a priest, you'd better be a good one" was all that Otto Schuler had to say when he heard of his son's wish. That statement contained the promise of both support and constructive criticism that only a family can give. Richard would maintain contact with his family throughout his years of study for the priesthood, drawing from them encouragement and an increased zeal to serve God's people.

Upon graduating from high school, Richard attended St. Thomas College in St. Paul, all the while keeping in mind his vocation, and forming friendships with those of his fellows who shared the same ambition. Playing the organ to finance his education and studying year-round, Richard earned the bulk of the requirements for his B.A. in English after just two years.

Now, at last, he was able to enter St. Paul's Seminary. After settling into his room on the first day, Richard put on his cassock and collar for the first time and looked at himself in the mirror. Soon he would be a priest he thought to himself. The year was 1940, and while the world plunged into war Richard plunged into the depths of the mystery of the Church. The seminary life was intense and somewhat removed from the world; here Richard broadened his intellectual life and his musical life, singing in the choir and—as always—playing the organ. After five years, ordination approached, and the candidates made their eight day silent retreat. As Richard prayed about his future, the future of the Church, and the future of the world during those days in August 1945 he could only guess from the sounds of celebration outside that the worst war in history had ended.

"*I leave you peace, my peace I give you*" (Jn. 14:27). The world hungered for the peace of Christ, and young Fr. Schuler heard the sounds of Peace in the music of the Church, music that was becoming increasingly important to his life as a priest. As a history and Latin teacher at Nazareth Hall Preparatory Seminary in Saint Paul for ten years, Fr. Schuler used his musical talents in the service of the school and the diocese, training choirs and directing a guild of Catholic organists. He decided early on that a career in secular music could not be reconciled with the demanding duties of a priest; also, sacred music had a unique character and purpose that seemed to touch upon his personal vocation.

During the summers of 1947-1950, on his own time and at his own expense, Fr. Schuler pursued a Master's degree at the prestigious Eastman School of Music in Rochester, New York. He earned an M.A. in music theory. As he reflected upon the history and structure of Church music, he grew to love more deeply the mystery and unity of the Church herself. Fr. Schuler's "romance" with the Church continued, and—like all lovers—he sought the presence of his beloved in all her fullness and beauty. Therefore he wanted to continue his studies in that great city where the Universal Church is most poignantly made visible; where Peter, who guarantees the Unity and Universality of the Church, shepherds a flock that stretches to the ends of the earth.

"That faith which is common to us both" (Rom. 1:12). Rome and the unity of faith—Fr. Schuler wished to be close to the center of the Church's life. He applied for a Fullbright Scholarship from the State Department to study music in Rome, and backed his application with intense prayer. He offered Mass in union with each of the saints in the Roman canon, the great Roman martyrs whose very lives were conformed to the Blood of Christ that he was presenting on the altar. With this offering he promised a pilgrimage to the church of each of these saints in Rome, praying there a rosary and meditating on the redemption in which each had shared.

"If anyone wishes to come after me, let him deny himself and take up his cross daily and follow me" (Lk. 9:23). The enrichment

of faith comes through the Cross, and Fr. Schuler's great pilgrimage of faith began and ended at the foot of the Cross. Even
as Fr. Schuler received his scholarship and prepared to go to
Rome, his father died. This left him with obligations to his wid-
owed mother, and the Archbishop suggested she accompany
him to Rome. Otto Schuler had taught his family to be devoted
to the Church, and though they were saddened by his death,
Rome offered an opportunity to be closer to that Church. And
so, in the fall of 1954, mother and son set off on their journey.

Rome brought an increase of faith through music, liturgy,
and the constant view of Peter feeding his sheep. Fr. Schuler
spent the year studying 15th and 16th century manuscripts at the
Vatican Library, and he was associated with the Pontifical Institute of Sacred Music and the State University of Rome. He also
attended every ceremony, beatification, or papal appearance
that he could. Through friends he was able to obtain an audience with Cardinal Ottaviani, who arranged for Fr. Schuler and
his mother to be present at Mass in the Sistine Chapel. Life in
Rome during the Pontificate of Pope Pius XII had a profound
influence in shaping and solidifying his appreciation of and
commitment to the Church, One, Holy, Catholic, and Apostolic.

But there is always the Cross. Every man has a natural desire to control the circumstances of his own life, to direct himself by his own choices. The priest, however, stands fully in the
Person of Christ, offering himself freely in obedience to the Father. Fr. Schuler returned from Rome in 1955 filled with a faith
that could move mountains. It seemed that no task would be too
difficult, no burden too great to bear as he awaited assignment
to his first parish. The Archbishop however, did not treat him
as he had expected—instead he assigned Fr. Schuler to teach at
St. Thomas College. This was not what he had hoped for; in fact
he feared that, because of some misunderstanding, he was being
disciplined for leaving the diocese and going to Rome.

Fr. Schuler nevertheless accepted his new tasks and embarked upon them with all the determination that he had. He

taught theology and music for the next fourteen years, thus continuing his service in the intellectual life. Moreover, he lived the life of a college professor, which gave him a certain freedom—freedom to further his education and establish contacts with members of the Church all over the world. Because of this flexibility Fr. Schuler was able to become significantly involved in the liturgical renewal, and more importantly his education and his "obedience of faith" enabled him to discern the spirits that were behind various trends in liturgy. The Holy Spirit was preparing him for his work at St. Agnes, moving his heart so that it would be sensitive to the call of the Church.

This preparation included a Ph.D. in musicology from the University of Minnesota, which Fr. Schuler completed in 1963. It was here that he became more involved with the larger musical world and furthered his own reputation as a musician and director of the first order. He also became involved in the Church Music Association of America, and began writing articles for its publication *Sacred Music*.

Meanwhile the same Spirit that was leading Fr. Schuler, inspiring in him deep devotion to the music of the Church, was also desiring to renew the whole life of that Church, and began by touching the humble heart of Pope John XXIII, who sought to promote renewal by calling for an Ecumenical Council. In doing so he initiated a drama of struggle between those who lived in the Spirit, Who *"searches the very depths of God"* (Rom. 8:27), and those who followed other spirits who *"changed the glory of the incorruptible God for an image made like to corruptible man ..."* (Rom. 1:23).

Fr. Schuler followed the Second Vatican Council with great interest, particularly the development of the Constitution on Sacred Liturgy. In that Constitution he heard a call for renewal in the liturgy, in order that the Eucharistic sacrifice might penetrate more deeply the whole of the Mystical Body. To further this end the Council called for "active participation" by all the faithful in the liturgy, and made allowance for new creativity and diversity in liturgical life, while at the same time insisting on the preservation of the venerable traditions and indeed for a greater appreciation of them. Development in continuity with the past; vernacular in addition to Latin; the beauty and simplicity of Gregorian chant along with any other music—old or new—that was both "sacred" and "art": Vatican II was a challenge to the Church to make liturgy more vital, more vivid in its reflection of the sacredness of the Eucharistic Sacrifice—the offering that bears fruit in the nourishment of men unto eternal life.

Fr. Schuler heard this challenge and responded with enthusiasm; for musicians and singers this challenge meant a greater love for the Gregorian chant, along with the charge to expand the corpus of Church music. This task carried with it a great responsibility: that this music preserve the character of "sacred art," as is proper to liturgical music, and without which it would be unable to fulfill its purpose.

Deeply conscious of this responsibility and now widely recognized for his ability in the field, Fr. Schuler accepted the honor and duty of being chairman of the Fifth International Church Music Congress that met at the close of the Council in 1965. It was here that he first sensed the coming crisis of faith that was to afflict so many in the Church, plunging them into confusion in the years that followed. Some at the Congress had clearly lost sight of the essence of the liturgy, and reflected this loss in their desire for a secularization of Church music. A spirit of novelty and experimentation, a spirit of individualism that reflected neither the character of the Mass nor the unity of the Church, was breaking forth in the liturgical movement, particularly in the United States. It spread from the liturgy to the whole of Church life, threatening the very identity of the Christian in the face of a world that was following *teachers who delighted their fancy* (2 Tm. 4:3).

Elected vice president of the papal federation of church music societies founded by Pope Paul VI, and as a member of the American bishops' advisory board on church music, Fr. Schuler was able to follow the developments around the world following the close of Vatican II. In the midst of the storm, he stood fast, determined to implement the renewal that the Church had called for. God had prepared him for this time, strengthened his faith, and imparted to him a sense of vision and a mission to prepare those entrusted to his care for a renewed outpouring of the Holy Spirit.

"Put on the armor of God" (Eph. 6:11). Msgr. Schuler was now outfitted for a new and especially demanding work—his loyal insight, his reading of the "signs of the times," gave him the discernment necessary to implement the Council in every facet of church life. Therefore, in 1969 he was called forth from the life of teaching and made pastor of the parish of St. Agnes. He now brought his lifelong love for the Church—his romance with a Bride whose beauty had grown only more vivid with the years—into a constant and absorbing service to the People of God. And the needs of his people—great and small—convinced him even more deeply of the Church's call; he saw in his daily parish duties a more concrete expression of the meaning of the priesthood.

St. Agnes is a large "national" parish with members all over the city of Austrian-Bavarian background. In addition to the pastorate, Msgr. Schuler became superintendent of St. Agnes elementary and high schools. The work with the schools was particularly difficult in the early years of his administration. During the early 1970's Msgr. Schuler found himself in a struggle for the control of the curriculum. The Diocesan Education Office had recommended certain textbooks of religion that contained fundamental errors. When Msgr. Schuler refused to use the texts in his schools, the Office attempted to pressure him through his own teachers and through various diocesan channels. He refused to be intimidated, however, insisting that the board did not have the authority to impose the texts. Ultimately his right of refusal was recognized. An important battle had been won, and the Catholicity of the curriculum was thus insured.

Further, Msgr. Schuler established his own certification program for teachers, steering them clear of programs constructed by bureaucratic offices that are often confused as to the nature of Catholic education. In these ways Msgr. Schuler fulfilled his duties as educator and priest, insuring that St. Agnes' schools remain today a mirror of the teaching Church, and that their administration, classrooms, and textbooks serve as a light to reveal that Church to young minds.

The students themselves, however, have at times been a source of trouble. At one point, some of the high school students threatened a "strike." Msgr. Schuler's response was straight-forward and firm—he simply informed the students that he would refund the tuition of any who wished to leave. The students saw that he had no intention of wavering in his authority, and the crisis was averted; moreover no one took him up on his offer.

"And you will find rest for your souls, for my yoke is easy and my burden light" (Mt. 11:30). Parish work, despite the trials brought about by the confusion of the contemporary situation, has brought many consolations. The parishioners of St. Agnes have eagerly shared in Msgr. Schuler's vision of liturgical life. According to the New Order of the Mass with its prescribed ritual and the use of Latin, Msgr. Schuler celebrates a Latin High Mass each Sunday. He has gathered dedicated singers in the area into the Twin Cities Catholic Chorale, and he directs them in a variety of church music, from Gregorian chant to the great masses of Mozart, Haydn, Beethoven, and Schubert which they present along with members of the Minnesota Orchestra on thirty Sundays each year. Also, Msgr. Schuler has served as president of the Church Music Association of America since 1975, and edits the quarterly magazine *Sacred Music*, using it as a medium for the authentic renewal of the liturgical music he loves so greatly.

The Eucharistic sacrifice is the center and source of an active parish life. Msgr. Schuler sees his mission to parishioners as a fostering of the personal vocation to holiness that each possesses. The priest stands in the Person of Christ, and as such he is the vehicle through which the faithful are drawn into the mystery of Christ. The sense of this responsibility permeates every facet of his ministry. Whether he is preaching in the pulpit, exercising his "prophetic mission"; or imparting in the confessional the mercy of God to a prodigal son; or graduating a class of high school students; or leading a Corpus Christi procession on the church grounds, with 1000 people proclaiming the Word made Flesh and adoring His presence in the Eucharist; or involved with his music or other apostolic activities—Msgr. Schuler seeks to be another Christ, washing the feet of his disciples, searching for the lost sheep, teaching in the temple, dying on the Cross. Msgr. Schuler is very aware of the fact that the pastor's time belongs wholly to the parish he serves. This service, however, does not seclude him; on the contrary it strengthens his bond with the whole Church, so absorbed is he in the rhythm of her daily life.

Springing forth from this daily life have been significant contributions to the Universal Church. Following the 1976 Conference of the Episcopal Church in Minneapolis that authorized the ordination of women, Msgr. Schuler became acquainted with several Episcopal priests who were convinced that this decision was not good. He arranged an audience for two of them with Cardinal Seper, prefect of the Sacred Congregation for the Doctrine of the Faith, in Rome. Both of them desired conversion to the Catholic Church, along with their congregations, and ordination to the priesthood. Because of dissatisfaction with the Anglican communion, they were determined to seek full union with the Catholic Church. As a result of meetings with Cardinal Seper, Rome approved an "Anglican Use" by which entire Episcopal congregations could enter the Church as parishes, and their priests could be ordained priests and serve as pastors. The reunion of separated communities envisioned by Vatican II was thus served by the efforts of Msgr. Schuler. The "Anglican Use", however, still faces various difficulties in its application and organization, and therefore remains one of his areas of constant prayer and concern.

Msgr. Schuler also has worked for the whole Church by fostering vocations to the priesthood. Eight priests have been ordained from his parish since he became pastor, and he serves as a spiritual director for many young seminarians. Pursuing a priestly vocation in these difficult times can be full of frustration when so many, especially in seminaries, misrepresent the Gospel. Msgr. Schuler seeks to insure that these young men are granted a vision of the Church as she truly stands; he listens to their problems, helps them in their study, and invites them to share in the liturgical life of his parish, so that they might praise God in their joys and draw strength from Him in their sufferings in union with the parishioners of St. Agnes, who are so steeped in the renewal of the Church. Msgr. Schuler hopes that in this way these young men will hear the true voice of the Church, and become seeds of her renewal some day in their own parishes.

Msgr. Richard Schuler is in all things a man in love with the Catholic Church. It is a true love, one that cannot be clouded over by deceit or discouragement because it is constantly focused on the beloved in all her goodness—a goodness that has its source and its strength in the Lord Jesus Christ. He thus stands as a prophetic witness—a witness first and foremost because he hears the voice of God and seeks in his priesthood to present Jesus Christ in all His truth and power, Jesus who is Head of the Mystical Body present in the world today. Msgr. Schuler testifies to what he hears: in his music, in his preaching, in his work in the parish, in his concern for vocations, in the obedience of faith that underlies his response to the call of the Church and shapes his entire priesthood. And his witness continues today as he invites all to join in with the voice—the song—of the Church: *"Praise the Lord; Praise and exalt Him above all forever!"* (Dn. 3:61ff).

IV.
Msgr. William Smith

St. Joseph's seminary sits on a hill along Seminary Avenue, a street that winds its way up from the homes and stores, restaurants, bakeries, and delicatessens that gather together on the Hudson River to form Yonkers, New York. From its gold dome to its foundation stone, St. Joseph's radiates strength and permanence; if it could speak it would probably say to America, "The Church is here to stay!"

Yonkers touches the northern border of the Bronx, and though some people call it "the sixth borough" of New York City, it likes to assert its own identity—a sense of neighborhood community built on the shared perspective of the Polish, Italian, and Irish ethnic groups that make Yonkers their home. The flavor of Yonkers is tangible, like that extra spice you notice in the spaghetti sauce that tells you that the restaurant cook makes it the same way at home for his kids. At the same time there is that universal touch that is distinctive to New York, an area that has its eyes wide open to everything that is going on in the world.

All of these things are very much a part of St. Joseph's Seminary; the fact that it is a major institution in one of the most important Catholic dioceses in the world does not make it any less a part of the neighborhood. And the institution is re-flected substantially in the man who is its Dean; a man who has lived his whole life in the shadow of St. Joseph's, yet who also has a vital role to play in speaking to America on behalf of the Church that St. Joseph's serves.

"My vows to the Lord I will fulfill before all his people" (Ps. 116:12). Msgr. William Smith is a priest perhaps best known for being in the "hot seat" on critical issues in the public forum. In sensitive areas of medical ethics, abortion, and homosexuality he has represented the voice of the teaching Church, often on na-tional television and radio. Yet Msgr. Smith is a man who never intended to be a "celebrity" and who does not especially seek the public eye. He speaks on behalf of the Church—on behalf of the diocese he is pledged to serve, and in recognition of the duties inherent in the diocesan priesthood. Msgr. Smith is a man of duty; his sense of duty, though, is not some impersonal thing, but rather it stems from a profound sense of encountering Christ in the various and often unpredictable circumstances that form the substance of his vocation.

Becoming the Dean of St. Joseph's Seminary was perhaps the last thing that William Smith would have predicted while growing up in Yonkers. Born on August 4, 1939, the youngest of three boys, William's family was characterized by quiet but steady devotion, a sense of duty to the Church and the obliga-tions of life, and a share in the values of a heavily Catholic neighborhood. *"The Lord alone was their leader, no strange god was with him"* (Deut. 32:12). William has nothing but fond mem-ories of a supportive childhood, one marked in particular by a great deal of intimacy with the parish priests, who frequently visited the Smith home. The priests were seen as members of the family, like "uncles" who seemed to play as much a part in the family upbringing and formation as anyone else. Every-where young William turned he saw a unity of influence and activity, despite the everyday problems that are part of the lives of everyone. "The home, the school, and the Church," the three basic sources of his personal growth, "were all playing the same tune, resonating the same values, confirming and reconfirming the same direction."

St. Denis parish played a large part in his boyhood years. Msgr. Joseph O'Connor, the pastor since 1921, was a revered and saintly man. His associates were often youthful and close to the children. All three of the Smith brothers were altar boys, and William thus had the opportunity to get to know the priests in a particularly intimate way. Often, Fr. Quill and Fr. Marshall would take William and some of the other boys on outings as a reward for doing the early Masses that no one else wanted to do. By third grade, William had already begun to think that he wanted to be just like these dedicated and friendly men whom he saw every day. *"Everyone should see how unselfish you are. The Lord is near"* (Phil. 4:4-5). William was attracted to the priesthood in a very concrete fashion; he wanted to imitate these priests because he saw in their lives something profound, a deep commitment underlying the variety of their service.

After grade school, William attended Xavier High School, run by the Society of Jesus. Here he learned Latin and Greek, played sports, and became involved in charitable activities. The Jesuits too were exemplary, yet William still felt drawn to the parish life, though he could not give detailed reasons why. As graduation approached and he determined to enter the diocesan seminary, he remembers that "I became the object of a vocations campaign" by the ever-zealous Jesuits. "Why don't you want to be a Jesuit," they asked him, "and oddly enough I kept saying I didn't want to be a teacher." The diversity of the parish duties, their intimate connection with daily life, attracted him and called upon him to commit himself to a kind of service defined solely by the day to day requirements of the Church and the needs of the people. *"Do not live in fear, little flock. It has pleased your Father to give you the kingdom"* (Lk. 12:32). The parish priest, he realized, serves as that intimate and necessary link between the Catholic people and the teaching, ruling, and sanctifying aspects of their Church. When William graduated from high school in 1957, the Church, under Pope Pius XII, reflected deeply the solidarity of all her members. This reflection formed the whole of William's boyhood experience and solidified his vocation; the Church in his early life seemed to be one large team, "some people were guards and some were ends, but there was no question where that goal line was."

At this time, however, his understanding was more practical than theoretical. William devoted a good deal of time to following the statistics of the New York Yankees, and at first, things such as *Mystici Corporis* and *Humani generis* sounded like names of diseases to him. A fellow student at Cathedral College, James O'Connor, was by contrast quite interested in these weighty theological matters. The two began by being on opposite sides of various discussions and arguments, but their relationship quickly developed into a friendship that lasted throughout their seminary years and indeed to this very day as colleagues on the faculty. After two years of general studies at Cathedral, the students made their dramatic entrance into the formidable seminary of St. Joseph.

In the year 1959, such an entrance brought a seminarian into a world of unparalleled discipline and regimentation. From 5:30 in the morning until 10:00 at night, every minute was accounted for, divided among prayer, classes, study, and recreation. It seems that the object of the regimentation and order was to keep a seminarian from performing any one activity for too long. This training would then carry over into parish life, which—although structurally different from seminary life—nevertheless is characterized by constantly changing demands on a priest's attention. The seminary structure was designed to give the priest the discipline and flexibility for this kind of life.

"The Lord is great and worthy to be praised in the city of our God" (Ps. 48:1). If a seminarian was at peace with himself and sure of his goal, he could make it through the system, have

a sense of humor about it, even thrive on it. Msgr. Smith insists, "I *enjoyed* my time at the seminary in as much as I was doing exactly what I wanted to do all the time every day, although if you judged it by contemporary standards it was a little bit stricter than Sing Sing prison!" All kidding aside, however, the strictness was not slavish in that it was informed with a clear purpose, and lived not only by the students but also by the priests who comprised the faculty. Hence "what to outsiders may have looked like a burden was actually a system of providential ways to maximize your time and your personal development."

In addition, each class of seminarians developed their own special bond of solidarity and friendship from the sharing of common activities and the achievement of a common goal. William's class, however, was particularly noteworthy because of a unique and ongoing event that dominated his years of theological study.

On October 11, 1962 the seminarians at St. Joseph's were granted fifteen extra minutes of recreation, something that was not often done. This, however, was no ordinary day, for the entire seminary was gathered around a television set to watch the opening of the Second Vatican Council. The occasion was one of great solemnity, yet when the secular television commentator announced that "the choir is now going to sing 'Come CREATED Spirit' " the seminarians roared with laughter.

For the next few years, the seminarians followed the Council with enthusiasm, "like a World Series in motion." St. Joseph's dogma professor, Fr. Austin Vaughan, was a man of towering stature both intellectually and spiritually. Digesting the daily reports of *L'Observatore Romano*, Fr. Vaughan would recapitulate for each class the action on the Council floor the previous day. In this way, William's class was trained to assimilate the authentic teaching of Vatican II—viewed in continuity with the whole of the Church's tradition—even while that teaching was being formed. Another important influence on William personally was Msgr. Daniel Flynn, who not only trained him to be an altar boy as a youth, but also taught him almost all of his moral theology in the Seminary.

Finally the much anticipated ordination day arrived on May 28, 1966. William was deeply moved by the ceremony at St. Patrick's Cathedral, with his family present and Cardinal Spellman, just back from the Council, imposing the hands that stretched forth through their consecration from the hands of the very apostles themselves. As members of the first class to be ordained after the close of Vatican II, William and his fellows had particular obligations toward the renewal of the Church. (Msgr. Smith remarks that, "As I often point out to Fr. Curran, he's pre-Vatican II, I'm not.")

"He who calls us is trustworthy" (1 Thes. 5:24). The new Father Smith became assistant pastor at St. Francis Church in Mt. Kisco, north of Yonkers. Here he delved into the parish life just as he had always hoped he would, ministering to a growing and active hospital, teaching the children in school, giving sermons, and administering the sacraments. He had immediately been placed in that formative role that so influenced him as a child. Fr. Smith quickly learned about the trust that people put in the Church. Here he was, young and unknown, coming into a parish and taking a directive role in people's lives, some of whom had been Catholics since long before he was born. They did not know him, but they trusted the Church who sent him.

This in turn gave a tremendous sense of responsibility to the young priest. Fr. Smith wondered how God could place such an important matter in the hands of someone so young as himself, but he realized that, many years ago, a young woman in Nazareth was entrusted with the task of bearing the Word-made-flesh. Indeed, God has a great deal of confidence in young people who are devoted to Him.

Fr. Smith was nevertheless prepared to take on any other task at the call of the bishop. He was already aware of the possibility that he might end up teaching in the seminary; while still a seminarian, some of his professors had "sounded him out" about the possibility of an academic career. Although at that time he admitted that he had no desire to be a teacher, he nevertheless pledged his loyalty to the wishes of the bishop.

Now the will of New York's new bishop, Terence Cardinal Cooke, became clear. At the recommendation of St. Joseph's seminary faculty, Fr. Smith was to pursue advanced studies in moral theology with a view to becoming involved in seminary life. After an interim year of teaching religion at Stepinac High School, Fr. Smith got his passport and prepared to go to Rome, along with Fr. O'Connor, who was studying dogmatic theology, and all the other priests from the Archdiocese of New York who were being sent to pursue doctoral degrees.

As with everything else, however, a diocesan priest can never be sure of his travel plans. Cardinal Cooke had just been placed on the board of directors of the Catholic University of America, as is common for prominent members of the American hierarchy. The president of the school complained to the Cardinal that "New York never sends us anyone unless there's a war on," referring to the Archdiocese's policy of sending its students to Rome. Cardinal Cooke, realizing that there was one particular priest that he could send to Washington, D. C., replied, "Well, we're sending one right now." Thus Msgr. Smith recalls that, when the semester started, "I found myself going down the New Jersey Turnpike, which is not the way to Rome."

"I do not run like a man who loses sight of the finish line" (Cor. 9:25). It was the fall of 1969, and when the priest-student arrived at the Catholic University he soon discovered that "the silly season had emerged" in the school of theology. *Humanae vitae* was a year old, and some of the professors were no doubt *wishing* that this encyclical would go away. The theology school was polarized over the issue of dissent. Fr. Smith was deeply disturbed by the "politicization" of the faith; the idea that one had to choose sides "for" or "against" Catholic teaching at a Catholic

university was to him ridiculous. It was as if the team were breaking apart and the players running all over the field.

"He has kept my soul from death, my eyes from tears, and my feet from stumbling" (Ps. 116:8). Fr. Smith quickly realized that his loyalty to the Church and defense of her teaching would cause him difficulty with the dissenters on the faculty. Recognizing that he had been sent to the university for a specific purpose, Fr. Smith dug in his heals and set about getting his degree as quickly as possible, determined not to compromise the Church, but also determined not to allow those who were abandoning their loyalty to the Church to have any excuse to hinder him from accomplishing the task that the bishop had given him. His call was to the formation of seminarians; there would be plenty of battles to be fought and a great deal to be learned after he had his doctorate of Sacred Theology. Thus he determined to make his stay at the university as short and as smooth as fidelity to his principles would allow.

"The Word is near you, on your lips and in your heart" (Rom. 10:8). Through two turbulent years at Catholic University Fr. Smith kept a low profile and fulfilled his academic requirements. Upon receiving his degree, Fr. Smith attained a status far different than he had ever expected. He was now a Moral Theologian, thrust forth in the midst of a crisis. The Church once again placed great trust in him, and he was determined to represent her teachings with faithfulness, through the power of the Spirit of God.

And there was yet another trust that he was about to receive from God. The formation of His priests, the delicate nurturing of personal vocations as they correspond to that highest call of the Lord through His Church, to be conformed to Him in the fullness of His redemptive action: a task such as this carries a tremendous responsibility, particularly in these difficult years. Fr. Smith, however, was prepared because he saw this task, like all others, as a fulfillment of his duty.

The duty of a diocesan priest is unique because it does not correspond to a particular charism; rather it is universal within the local circumstances of a parish or other diocesan service. The priest makes the bishop "present" locally to his people; he participates in the bishop's duty of shepherding the flock. This means the willingness to accept a variety of assignments and, within each assignment, the variety of responses that each circumstance requires.

Fr. Smith identifies this unpredictable variety as "both the beauty and the challenge of the diocesan priesthood; whoever knocks on the door, you answer the door." The duty of a diocesan priest can be expressed as "opening the door." A parish priest in a rectory hears knocking all during the course of the day, and on the other side of his front door he might find anyone from the local mayor to a transient who needs money or food to a kid from the neighborhood. Despite the variety of people, needs, and situations, however, there is a profound underlying consistency—it is on the other side of that open door that the priest finds, each and every time, the person of Jesus Christ.

For Fr. Smith, the knock on the door was a call away from the parish life he loved and into a seminary where he could communicate that love to others. He knew that it was Christ who called, Christ who was on the other side of the door of his heart. In 1971, he answered that door, becoming professor of Moral Theology at St. Joseph's seminary.

"What we have seen and heard we proclaim in turn to you so that you may share life with us" (1 John 1:2). Fr. Smith had never imagined himself as a teacher, but seminary teaching is much different from a college professorship. At the seminary, he is "teaching his own", playing a vital role in enriching the ministry of the diocese. Also there is a strong pastoral component to seminary teaching; by knowing what the Church expects of her priests and integrating it with his own life, Fr. Smith is able to communicate the essence of that openness that characterizes the

diocesan priestly vocation. In addition, the current situation has created its own special difficulties. Many young men come to the seminary without a clear knowledge of the essentials of the faith. This means that there is an added need for communication between the faculty and the seminarians. *"Righteous and true are your ways"* (Rev. 15:3). Theology embraces a way of life, and it is essential both for the sake of fidelity to the Gospel and for the happiness and stability of the candidate that he be at peace with what the Church teaches. "Better to talk out a problem here than live it out later on," Fr. Smith points out.

Thus St. Joseph's seminary has maintained its own "peace" as an institution dedicated to the Gospel during a time when some other seminaries in America are tossing about in a sea of irrelevant novelty and a crippling lack of discernment. Soon after Fr. Smith's arrival as a professor, now-Bishop Vaughan became Rector of the seminary, bringing his lucid sense of the Church and its authentic renewal into the administration of St. Joseph's.

This particular seminary thus has had an important role not only in training its own priests, but also in representing the teaching Church. As the 1970's wore on, issues of ethics became prominent in New York politics and in the national public forum. The Archdiocese of New York was continually called upon to present the teaching of the Church, often to a hostile, secular audience. Cardinal Cooke needed an articulate and knowledgeable spokesman who could grapple with issues that were having a serious impact on American public life, as well as a confusing effect on the faithful. There was a knock on the seminary door, and Fr. Smith answered.

"I am for peace, but when I speak, they are for fighting" (Ps. 120:7). Under Cardinal Cooke and his successor Cardinal O'Connor, Fr. Smith has spoken for the Church on a variety of moral topics, proclaiming the Gospel even in the most unfavorable circumstances. He has appeared on national television programs, including the Today Show, Phil Donahue, David

Suskind, 20/20, First Estate, Good Morning America, Firing Line, and Cable Network News, and has also written numerous articles and given important lectures.

His involvement in the public realm of ideas and issues convinced Fr. Smith more and more that the Word of God, particularly as it is expressed in the intellectual apostolate, was frequently misunderstood and increasingly unpopular. Loyal Catholic thinkers abounded, but they were isolated from one another, forced to face hostile forces in the world—even in the Church—alone. The burden of this situation could become too great for some to bear. "There's always the danger that you'll be shaving one morning and you'll think, 'Maybe *I'm* the one who's crazy!' " This realization prompted Fr. Smith and several other concerned intellectuals to found the Fellowship of Catholic Scholars in order to provide a sense of solidarity in the midst of crisis, reminiscent of the great sense of teamwork he remembered so well from his youth. *"Don't be conquered by evil but conquer evil with good"* (Rom. 12:21). Fr. Smith served as president from 1981 to 1983.

"He has spoken to us through His Son" (Heb. 1:2). In all of his activities as seminary professor, whether proclaiming the teachings of the Church or dealing directly with his seminarian students, Fr. Smith sees that same consistency-within-diversity that characterizes parish life: "Whatever comes up, comes up, and you deal with it." A seminary priest, or a parish priest, or any priest in the diocese simply has to examine every task, break it into manageable parts, and go to work; keeping in mind at all times a supernatural vision, a conviction of the reality and primacy of the spiritual. This means seeing Jesus Christ in the substance and at the end of every priestly duty. *"It pleased God to make absolute fullness reside in him and, by means of him, to reconcile everything in his person"* (Col. 11:19). Such a vision is impossible without three components that Fr. Smith continually stresses to his students and to anyone who will listen: sound doctrine, in order to *know* Jesus Christ; sound interior life, in order

to encounter Christ in prayer and the sacraments, increasing *love* and union with Him; and sound personal practice, in order to *serve* Christ as He presents Himself in the demands of priestly life.

Jesus Christ is the goal and Jesus Christ is found everywhere, linked as He is to the destiny of every human being. Therefore it is impossible for a faithful priest to be idle. "Go visit the sick or teach some kids the Hail Mary," Fr. Smith would say to priests who find time on their hands. "No honest priest would say that he has *nothing* to do." Nevertheless, the devoted parish priest often serves with a zeal known only to God, and even if he does become a celebrity in the course of his duties, his ultimate successes are usually hidden ones: "Some of the most important things we work at will never show up in a cost/benefit analysis, nor in a book, nor in a glossy magazine," Fr. Smith observes. The greatest deeds, done to Jesus in the persons and situations that plant themselves on the front doorstep of the diocesan priest, are written only in the Book of Life. *"O search me, God, and know my heart"* (Ps. 139:24).

Fr. Smith, with his strong sense of the meaning of the priesthood, and his recognized status within the intellectual community, was the ideal choice for Dean of the Seminary in 1977. His approach to theology is professional and scholarly but at the same time embraces the full sense of "faith seeking understanding." Knowing that "if theology were sheerly knowledge, it could be done by a correspondence course," Fr. Smith tries to integrate knowledge with life, so that his candidates increase in *wisdom*. *"Draw close to God, and He will draw close to you"* (Jas 4:7).

In addition to his seminary work, Fr. Smith helps out in various other works within the diocese; he assists at Immaculate Heart of Mary parish in Scarsdale, New York on Sundays, works as Vice-Chancellor of the Archdiocese during the summer, and serves as chaplain for the South Bronx house of the Missionaries of Charity, a work which brought him to Calcutta,

India to preach retreats to Mother Teresa and her sisters during Christmas of 1983.

Finally, it was in recognition of his service that, at the recommendation of Cardinal O'Connor, Pope John Paul II conferred the title of Monsignor upon William Smith in March of 1986. This honor singles out Msgr. Smith for his loyalty to the Church and loyalty to duty. During his twenty years in the priesthood of Jesus Christ, he has answered the door for parishioners, high school students, seminarians, religious, the inquiring secular press, and—always—the Cardinal Archbishop of New York. One might say that the door, so often used, is simply left open, lest the appearance of Christ with His ever-present call might for a moment be obscured. And most often it is young men who walk through the passageway, following the same Christ, who has brought them to St. Joseph's Seminary to become His priests. For these, Msgr. Smith has one especially important message, a message he has tried to live: "Wherever you are assigned by the Bishop as a diocesan priest really does not matter too much, but what matters very much is that we be faithful. If it involves some public attention or no notice at all, what difference? St. Luke's gospel tells us what makes the difference and what really matters: 'We have done no more than our duty' " (Lk. 17:10).

V.
Abbot Ladislas K. Parker, O. Praem.

Night has fallen and the cross of the Abbey church nearly touches the stars of the evening sky. There are only the sounds of a waterfall in the garden and the soft footsteps of men in white robes entering the church from either side. The hour is Compline, and the members of the community of St. Michael's Abbey are gathering to thank the Lord for the blessings of the day and to ask Him for a restful night. Inside the church, the silence is penetrated harmoniously by the lifting of voices in song. As they chant the psalms of the Divine Office, these priests meditate on a calling which has linked their destiny to the community of this Abbey and to the Order of Premontre. *"In the great congregation I will bless the Lord"* (Ps. 26:12).

This Order takes its character from St. Norbert, its founder, who in the 12th century had a vision of a community of priests living both the prayer life of monks and the preaching and teaching life of apostles. It is a life founded on an attitude of continual conversion of heart through prayer and penance, a conversion that flows forth from each member and nourishes a genuine and continuous renewal of the entire People of God.

On this night at St. Michael's Abbey, one is struck by the sense of the timeless value of this commitment; it is constant and at the same time uniquely relevant to the situations in which it is brought to bear. The scene could be medieval France, 17th century Austria, or 20th century Hungary. But instead, by virtue of the call of God and the dedicated cooperation of a handful of men, the vision of St. Norbert thrives here at the foot of the Santa Ana mountains in California and stretches forth over Orange County, Los Angeles, and the whole of the United States of America.

"I will walk with integrity of heart within my house" (Ps. 101:2). Among the brethren of St. Michael's, there is one who stands alone in responsibility; the one who is called—with reverence and affection—Father Abbot. Father Ladislas K. Parker is a man whose distinctive qualities shine forth whether he is in the choir, in the refectory, or walking the Abbey grounds. Fr. Parker radiates sensitivity, devotion, and courage, embodying the history and destiny of an Abbey that reflects in itself the drama of the 20th century—the endurance of the Gospel against both the atheism of the East and the materialism of the West.

"Behold, evil is going forth from nation to nation, and great tempest is stirring from the farthest parts of the earth" (Jer. 25:32). The Holy Spirit would shape Fr. Parker's life so that it would manifest the peace of Christ in the midst of turmoil. Therefore it was not ironic that his life should begin in the middle of a war that shook Europe to its foundations. Ladislas Parker was born in the Empire of Austria-Hungary on December 19, 1915. His father was a farmer and wine grower by trade, but circumstances had made him—like his entire generation—a soldier in the army of Emperor Franz Joseph. Ladislas would never know his father, who was killed in what the people of the day called "the Great War," a victim of the senselessness of man's rebellion against God and the hatred and conflicts that are its fruits. Nevertheless, Ladislas did know a peaceful child-

hood. Though he was the first and only child, his mother did not remarry; instead his grandparents came to their farm in West Hungary—very near the Austrian border. His grandfather, a blacksmith, provided the family with an income against the day when Ladislas would manage the vineyard for himself.

His career, it seemed, was determined, but Ladislas began to show signs very early that the Lord was drawing him to His own vineyard. *"Behold, I have put my words in your mouth"* (Jer. 1:9). At age 5, his mother would take him to church and the young boy would be fascinated by the style and manner of the preacher. Back at home, Mother would turn the kitchen stool upside down, like a pulpit, and place little Ladislas inside, where he would imitate the gestures and expressions of the priest giving a sermon.

Here already was the beginning of Ladislas's deep appreciation of priestly service. When he grew older, he served at the altar early in the morning every day, even during the summer. On Sundays his grandfather, prayerbook and hymnal in hand, would beam with pride as he watched his grandson's meticulous devotion in assisting the priest.

Ladislas loved to serve Mass, and in retrospect he is convinced that a longing for the priesthood was subconsciously present in that love, even while he was a small boy. As he grew, the longing became recognizable to him, and by the age of eleven he was convinced that he wanted to be a priest himself, yet he kept this conviction secret—he was, after all, being prepared to manage a farm. *"I rise before dawn and cry for help. I hope in thy words"* (Ps. 119:147).

The family spoke German, and it seemed wise to his grandparents that Ladislas go to school in Budapest so that he could learn Hungarian and thus be more successful in the new post-war Hungarian Republic of which he was now a citizen. While in Budapest, however, one of his teachers saw in Ladislas a profound potential for learning, particularly in the areas of languages, history, and religion. The teacher came home with

Ladislas after that year, and met with his mother and grandparents. He was able to convince them that Ladislas would be wasting his potential on the farm, that he belonged in the gymnasium (high school) of the Norbertine fathers. His grandfather, remembering the diligence and faith of Ladislas at the altar of God, saw the will of the Holy Spirit in this advice. "We will find another way to manage the vineyard," he said with resignation, and Ladislas set out for high school and the discovery of the charism of St. Norbert, a vision that would correspond to and reveal more fully the secret hope he held in his own heart.

At high school, Ladislas excelled in studies and proved himself a leader among his classmates. At the same time he saw a unique quality in the priests who were his teachers; the devotion they showed for him and his peers was an inspiration, and reflected an aspect of the priestly ministry that is particularly Norbertine—working with the youth. *"Whoever receives one such child in my name receives me"* (Mk. 9:37). Though still young himself, Ladislas grasped the essential element of this mission; he realized the importance of youth both for the country and the Church, and the corresponding importance of forming them correctly—teaching them the truths of the Gospel and the world that God has created.

Priest and teacher—this was the emerging ambition of young Ladislas. By his sophomore year in high school he had made up his mind to join the Order of Premontre, embracing the eight hundred year tradition of St. Norbert. He told no one of his decision, but soon it was no longer necessary to reveal his intention, for all who knew him could see that he was headed in that direction; the students who elected Ladislas student body president in his senior year fully expected that one day he would sit on the other side of the classroom desk.

Therefore it surprised no one that, on August 9, 1935—the Feast of the Transfiguration—Ladislas Parker entered the Abbey of St. Michael at Csorna as a novice. The Abbey at Csorna was almost as old as the Order itself, having been founded in 1180 and having endured a good deal of secular interference, suppression, and political upheaval. *"The Lord is my Rock, and my fortress, and my deliverer"* (Ps. 18:2). At this time, the Abbot was Ladislas's former high school principal, and the novice's career seemed as though it would follow along the same academic lines as he had pursued in high school. The Abbot was determined that Ladislas would do graduate study in German and Latin literature in preparation for teaching in his old high school.

This direction, however, changed abruptly—in a way that would prove to be much more significant than anyone could have imagined at the time. The Abbot General of the Order in Rome had noted with concern that only one member of the Csorna Abbey was pursuing theological study in a Roman university. He indicated that St. Michael's should send at least one more candidate to Rome. Viewing the intellectual promise of Ladislas, who had just taken simple vows and completed his philosophy in 1937, the Abbot of Csorna decided that Ladislas should postpone his advanced studies in literature and pursue theology at the Gregorian university.

"Heaven and earth will pass away but my words will never pass away" (Mt. 24:35). In theology Ladislas discovered a lifelong love. After his first year of study he begged the Abbot to allow him to specialize in theology instead of literature, and the Abbot agreed. Ladislas found himself exploring the richness of the mysteries of the faith, and in so doing he also found a new dimension to his vocation. The Norbertine life has its basis in community prayer, and its activity should be the fruit of the contemplation that is fostered by the monastic tradition. Theology deepened Ladislas's appreciation of his faith, and with this came a thirst for prayer and union with God. The community life reflected the life of the whole Church, a life steeped in the offering of Jesus to the Father, drawing all men to Himself. Thus Ladislas saw his vocation taking root in the community liturgy and the chanting of the Divine Office; and by solemn

profession in 1939 he was forever linked to his brethren at St. Michael's Abbey in Csorna. He had already developed a profound sense of the relationship between his own vocation and the vitality of that bond.

A year later, on August 20, Ladislas K. Parker was ordained priest in the Abbey of Csorna. He returned to Rome for two more years of study culminating in his reception of the doctorate of Sacred Theology, *Magna Cum Laude*, in 1943. He then returned to the Abbey and immediately found himself in a leadership role, teaching Moral Theology, Metaphysics, and Ethics, and—within a year—taking on the duties of novice master.

These were times of relative freedom for the Church in Hungary. Of course, a hideous threat had darkened the face of Europe, and war had descended once again upon her people. Hungary was allied with the vicious regime of Adolph Hitler during the war, but for political rather than ideological reasons. Meanwhile the Germans themselves did not gain real power in Hungary, and the Church was spared from the worst of the Nazi brutalities.

Nevertheless the Church and the Gospel needed strong defenders and courageous apostles, and Fr. Parker was keenly aware of the challenge this presented to the teaching apostolate. It was a Norbertine tradition to educate men for the work of evangelization, and Fr. Parker and his Abbey made this their goal. Already in Hungary, graduates of Csorna's educational formation were displaying the light of truth in a variety of services to the Church both inside and outside of the Order. Fr. Parker remembers in particular one diocesan pastor—educated at the Abbey in the early part of the century—who was noteworthy for his effectiveness, steadfastness, and zeal. Joseph Mindzenty's qualities would soon bring him to the episcopate and the College of Cardinals, and would also prepare him for the trials that lay ahead, trials that neither he nor Fr. Parker could have anticipated.

"In the path where I walk they have hidden a trap for me" (Ps. 142:3). In 1945, however, the first hint of these approaching trials was perceptible only to the most discerning of men. The victorious Red Army and its Hungarian partisans swept through the country, presenting themselves as liberators and agents of reconciliation and social peace. An announcement preceded them: "Priests and policemen stay in your place, we need you!" From 1945-1947 the victorious Communists formed a coalition government with other political movements, and it appeared as though the Church would be left alone, perhaps even treated with respect.

Fr. Parker, however, had observed the behavior of Communists in other countries where they had gained power, and he was convinced that the "olive branch" was nothing more than a clever ploy to buy time while the Communists consolidated their control. He also knew that it was essential to the Communist consolidation to capture the minds and hearts of the youth, and therefore it would only be a matter of time before the Norbertines and all other teaching orders would be crushed by the secular power. He thus began to conceive in his own mind, and to discuss with several others, a plan for a center outside the country where the Order of Premontre could be sustained and increased until the day when the Communist occupation of Hungary had ended and the Norbertines could return to effective work inside the country.

Fr. Parker's realism sprang from his understanding that the motivating forces behind Communism were completely opposed to the Good News of Jesus Christ. In its atheism Communism is anti-God, and in its materialism it is anti-man. Fr. Parker knew that the Communist ideology attacked the very fundamentals of Christianity—the loving call of a personal God and the dignity of the human person who receives that call, his spiritual nature, and his destiny to partake of the Divine life. He was convinced that the initial gestures of conciliation and tolerance would give way to persecution. *"Beware of a scoundrel for he devises evil, lest he give you a lasting blemish"* (Sir. 11:33).

In 1948 things began to change abruptly: opposition political parties were outlawed and Cardinal Mindzenty was arrested. Workers were herded into "party seminars" where they were indoctrinated in the philosophy of Feuerbach and Hegel—God was presented as the product of man's imagination, the projection of his own fears and ambitions. God Himself had been proven a myth, the party said, by the findings of modern science.

In response to such teaching, Fr. Parker prepared a series of sermons dealing with two fundamental questions: "Is there a God?" and "Do we have an immortal soul?". He was determined to expound the teaching of theology, philosophy, and true science on the evolution of man: that the spiritual element in man constitutes the fullness of his dignity, and could not possibly have "evolved" from the material. Man is utterly distinct from the rest of material creation in his origin and in his end. On Septuagesima Sunday, 1950, Fr. Parker gave the first of these sermons at 11:00 Mass in the Abbey church. Not all of his audience was sympathetic, however, and when one of his anecdotes was misinterpreted as an attack against Stalin, he was reported to the local police. Fr. Parker was called in for questioning and warned not to "jeopardize" good relations between Church and State. He was now a marked man.

During Lent of 1950, Fr. Parker was invited to give a retreat in a parish near the Austrian border. The secret police followed him and, after listening to his first talk in which he defended the immortality of the soul, they rounded him up and sent him back to the Abbey. His speeches, they said, were "undemocratic." The pastor protested interference in Church affairs, but to no avail.

"When they persecute you in one town, flee to the next" (Mt. 10:23). Abbot Eugene Simonffy told Fr. Parker at this time to devote himself exclusively to the teaching work, but it was only

a matter of time before this too would become unsafe. In June of 1950, 34 priests from the teaching orders were arrested; they were eventually released but the Communists had crafted a new condition in Church-State "relations"—only those priests already involved in parish work would be allowed to continue to function as priests. The schools were to be closed, and their staffs dispersed; priest-teachers would be assigned to the labor force where they could be "productive." The Communists were now unmasked—religion was to be relegated to the past and the souls of the young—through the schools—would henceforth belong to them!

Fr. Parker had prepared himself for this moment. He and the other seminary professors at the Abbey of St. Michael in Csorna now could no longer even serve as priests in the country. It was time to put his plan into action. The teachers and their novices would escape from Hungary and go to an English speaking country where they would serve God in community life and learn the English language. When the crisis had passed, they would return to Csorna and start an English speaking college there. Exile would be 5 or 6 years at the most; Fr. Parker could not imagine that the world would permit the Communists to terrorize his country for any length of time—eventually the free world would join forces and "roll back" the Iron Curtain. With this plan and with confidence in God, Fr. Parker approached the Abbot.

"Because of the danger of the proposal I cannot command you to do it, but you have my blessing." With these words Abbot Eugene laid his hand upon his novice master and several associates who were with him. It was the last guidance—and the last blessing—that they would ever receive from him.

Armed with their confidence that the escape attempt was indeed God's will, they went among their confreres seeking fellow travelers. Seven of the seminary professors, including Fr. Parker, were determined to risk the journey. None of the novices, however, were willing to go at this time; many had close family ties in Hungary and opted to hope for better times. Others were determined to observe the fate of the first band of escapees, and then follow. Still others already found themselves detained by the police; for them it was too late for escape. The community-in-exile would have to begin without novices, and as events unfolded it became apparent that those who had hoped to follow would be unable to do so.

The company complete, the seven priests planned their escape, selecting a particularly difficult stretch of terrain in the hopes that no one would expect an escape through such a route. On the night of July 11th, the Feast of St. Norbert, the Abbey received word that the police were to arrive the next morning to close them down and disperse the community. *"Do thou, O Lord, protect us, guard us ever from this generation"* (Ps. 12:7). The moment had come. At midnight, the seven split into two groups and headed for the border. No doubt St. Norbert and St. Michael were with them.

The way was littered with patrols, guards, and police. If caught they would no doubt be suspected of being spies, and would face lengthy interrogation, imprisonment, and perhaps torture. Yet the priests moved on, confident that God is more powerful than armies, and more subtle than the watchful eyes of evil men. *"Let my people go, that they may serve me"* (Ex. 9:13). They made their way across the fields, hiding in farmhouses while detachments of the border patrol marched by. The priests passed through a dense forest, and approached the border. Here they encountered a mine field and the Lord guided their feet. After this they cut through a barbed-wire fence, all the while combing the horizon for searchlights, listening for dogs or footsteps.

Between the fugitives and Austria there remained a sixty foot wide river and guards stationed in hidden places. The Lord stopped short of parting the waters for them, but He saw them across the river; they found a passage where the water came up only to their chins and thus they were able to walk slowly and silently across, stripped and holding their clothes above their heads. No one saw them. *"Thou didst give a wide place for my steps under me, and my feet did not slip"* (Ps. 18:36).

Only later did they discover that the guards had just returned from ten days of harvest and—being tired from their strenuous work—were sleeping quite soundly in the place where the seven crossed the border. A few weeks later a group of Cistercians were captured in that same area by a well-rested and more alert patrol. Austria did not, however, represent the end of danger for Fr. Parker and his confreres. They were in the Soviet occupied zone, about fifty miles from American controlled territory. Here one of their contacts, a local pastor, arranged for a pickup truck. Huddled and concealed in the back, they rode the final miles to freedom. *". . . by strength of hand the Lord brought you out from this place"* (Ex. 13:3).

The seven joined together in Vienna to praise God for their deliverance, and set off for Rome. Meanwhile St. Michael's Abbey was taken over by the government and its buildings were turned into a headquarters for the local soviet. The remaining Norbertines were dispersed and most had to take their priesthood underground. Abbot Eugene died in 1954 exiled from his flock by the world, but united to them in Christ Jesus.

Fr. Parker and his confreres were all that truly remained of St. Michael's Abbey as a visible corporate entity. This reality further fueled their determination to continue the Abbey's work on American soil. They had a special responsibility to their brethren in Hungary, as well as the entire suffering Church in Eastern Europe. God had granted them their freedom for a purpose, and in carrying out this purpose they—like their confreres behind the Iron Curtain—would be called upon to carry the Cross of Jesus Christ. *"He who loses his life for my sake will find it"* (Mt. 10:39).

With their goal thus before them, the fathers set out for America, borrowing $3000.00 to pay for their passage. They arrived in New York in 1952 with nothing but their clothes and their faith that all things are possible with God. The priests of St. Norbert's Abbey in DuPere, Wisconsin welcomed their exiled brethren with open arms. For a time, Fr. Parker taught moral theology at the Abbey seminary but he soon realized that his mission required him to seek another type of experience.

As the task of the seven became clear, Fr. Parker understood more fully why God had willed him to be a theologian. Realizing that their return to Hungary might not come as soon as they had initially expected, Fr. Parker saw that it was necessary for the Abbey to flourish anew in America. He was the only one of the seven with a doctorate in theology, which gave him the preparation he needed to establish a priestly formation and education program. What he now needed was more experience in pastoral ministry, so that he might develop the qualities necessary to lead a community effectively on a long-term basis. *"Train yourself in godliness"* (1 Tim. 4:7).

DuPere Abbey staffed a number of parishes in Montana, and Fr. Parker requested a position as a parish priest. The Abbot was determined to send him to a parish with a whole group of priests including several Norbertines, when suddenly one of Montana's small rural parishes found itself without its pastor, who had suffered a serious injury and faced six months in the hospital. Considering the needs of the people, and the ability and courage of Fr. Parker, the Abbot sent him to fill in for this parish . . . alone.

On a train crossing the midwestern United States, Fr. Parker struggled to translate his first sermon into English with the assistance of a German-English dictionary. Soon he arrived at his desolate parish; there was not even a housekeeper in the rectory.

"My eyes grow dim with waiting for my God" (Ps. 69:3). For the next several months Fr. Parker endured an intense loneliness and a longing for the community life to which he was called. Separated from his brothers and thousands of miles from the land of his home, struggling with a new language and a new

way of life, Fr. Parker would often stare out across the vast stretch of the plains and feel as though the sky was pressing him down against the ground. During this period of isolation he shared in the sufferings of his Norbertine brothers in Hungary whose own vocations to community life could no longer be followed. Together they formed one great communion of suffering, drawing close to the Heart of the Jesus who kept vigil alone in the Garden of Gethsemane.

Fr. Parker held fast to his faith in Christ, and his situation improved. He could, after all, still be a priest, and serve the people in his care. Soon the pastor was on his feet again, and Fr. Parker was able to move on to a parish with a group of priests. Here he kept contact with the other six members of St. Michael's who were scattered about from Wisconsin to France. They had all learned that distance did not sever the deep bonds that united them, nor keep their minds from the goal that they hoped to achieve. Saving the money that they earned in parish work, they built a financial base for their project of re-establishing a religious house so that they would be prepared when the right circumstances and location appeared.

These circumstances, under the direction of the Holy Spirit, began to take shape in 1957 when Cardinal McIntyre, archbishop of Los Angeles, invited all seven priests to teach at Mater Dei High School. The priests rejoiced at their reunion and at their opportunity to be involved once again in the specifically Norbertine apostolate of teaching the youth. During the next few years they searched the environs of Southern California for an appropriate and available piece of land.

"He brought me forth into a broad place" (Ps. 18:19). The area east of Los Angeles, toward the mountains, was at that time quite peaceful and quite undeveloped, and one day Fr. Parker happened upon a man who ran a small store and beer stand, and who owned 160 acres of land at the foot of Saddleback Mountain. He agreed to sell 34 acres and the priests, with their own finances and some generous donations, purchased the

property, mortgaged it, and used the bank money to put up the first two buildings. St. Michael's Priory was born.

Fr. Parker and his confreres were now ready to plunge into the task of forming priests for America's faithful. They had long been impressed by the quality of Catholicism in America—its uncomplicated sincerity and its intimacy; American lay people always expressed a deep and devoted—almost familial—love for the priests and nuns who educated them in their youth. The Hungarian priests hoped to recreate that atmosphere in their priory and cultivate the same kind of relationship with their seminarians and students. In 1961 Fr. Parker went to the senior classes at Mater Dei and spoke about the call and the charism of St. Norbert. Immediately he had four men for his novitiate. In 1962 the Junior Seminary opened and 29 young men from the diocesan school system signed on. As the Second Vatican Council approached, the fathers had high hopes; they did not expect the test that God had planned for them, and for the whole Church.

After the close of the Council, Fr. Parker adopted an attitude that effectively summed up its authentic program: "To hold steadfast to all that was good in the old and not to shy away either from that which is new." The reforms in religious life, including the establishment of a more consultative process of decision making, were embraced at St. Michael's according to the mind of the Church. Consultation meant more meetings for the superior, but it also meant that orders would be better understood and more zealously carried out. Such an approach would contribute to a greater sense of community solidarity without undermining the posture of obedience which in its deepest sense reflects the obedience of Christ.

"You have seen him, and it is he who speaks to you" (Jn. 9:37). The priests of St. Michael's knew the value of unity in their own lives, and therefore they appreciated its necessity for the Church as a whole. Faithful to the spirit of St. Norbert as well as the sense of the Universal Church, the priory was determined

to follow the teaching and direction of the Pope. Thus they did not fall victim to the curious and frightening malaise that seemed to seize hold of so many in the Church in the late 1960's. Some religious orders and congregations, under the pretext of reform, disregarded many of the traditions that were integral to the identity of their way of life. The end of the decade brought a crisis in religious life. Change without discernment had brought confusion to both young and old about the nature of a vocation that they had previously taken for granted. St. Michael's had remained steadfast, yet the disturbance of mind had crept in among the seminarians, and by 1967 they had lost all of the juniors and all of the candidates. The priory had shrunk to its original seven founders. *"When the Son of Man comes, will he find faith on earth"* (Lk 18:8)?

Fr. Parker reflects that this was the only time he was tempted to doubt whether their enterprise—the task and the goal that had sustained them throughout their period of exile—would truly succeed. But these were men who had faced adversity in the past and who had witnessed the power of the Holy Spirit; they gathered together—anxious but not afraid—and invoked "the big fighter St. Michael the Archangel, who knows the wiles of the Devil."

On the Feast of St. Michael, 1967, in the midst of a crisis of spirit that threatened to wreck the goal for which they had strived so long and hard, the fathers of St. Michael's priory in Orange, California conceived a fresh approach in their appeal for vocations. They presented St. Michael's as an institution specifically dedicated to the mind of the Church, the authentic and perennial sense of the vocation to religious life, a structured community prayer life, and an intellectual formation patterned after St. Augustine and St. Thomas Aquinas. St. Michael's priory proclaimed a special union with "the Vicar of Christ in his opposition to false interpretations of renewal."

"We are afflicted in every way, but not crushed" (2 Cor. 4:8). It was a daring step, and the priory was soon the object of criti-

cism from influential and vocal sources. Fr. Parker knew, however, that this criticism was rooted in infidelity and presented much less of a threat to the existence and flourishing of St. Michael's than would have resulted from the failure of the fathers to seize the moment and light a lamp for the truth of Christ.

And flourish they did! Candidates began appearing at the doorstep of St. Michael's Priory from all over the country; "refugees" from congregations or diocesan seminaries who were convinced that God was calling them to something that these institutions were failing to provide. Because of the courageous initiative of the fathers—the culmination of a lifetime of faithfulness to the Gospel in the midst of all manner of hostility, adversity, and confusion—God granted a special charism to the community of St. Michael, linking its very identity to the authentic revitalization of religious life. Men all over America who were drawn to life in the spirit of the evangelical counsels and according to the mission and ministry of St. Norbert were called by God to make a lifelong commitment to this religious community, transforming it into a model of renewed religious life.

Each year there were four or five new novices. Candidates took their theology in Rome, and soon there were new priests added to the community. Its apostolates expanded to a full residence high school, a summer camp attended each year by hundreds of boys aged 6-12, the staffing of the Hungarian-German parish of St. Steven in Los Angeles, and other assistance work in the dioceses of Orange and Los Angeles.

In 1984, with a community six times the size of the one that invoked St. Michael the Archangel on that pivotal day in 1967, the Abbot General of the Order of Premontre and Pope John Paul II approved the conferral of Abbey status on the community of St. Michael. Fr. Parker stepped forward to be invested as Abbot on September 20th. It had been thirty years since the community of St. Michael had had a leader whom they could call "Father Abbot." It had been a long struggle, a struggle that passed through the greatest evils of the present age, but also bore witness to the greatest good—the power of a God who is ever-faithful to His people.

Fr. Parker is not content to rest with this victory. He realizes that the Abbey stands for authentic religious life and fidelity to the Church, as well as being a monument to the millions whose voices have been silenced in Hungary and all over the world by an ideology and a persecution that is perhaps more virulent now than it was thirty-six years ago.

Nevertheless he faces the future with great hope, hope for America and for the Church. *"Faith is the assurance of things hoped for, the conviction of things not seen"* (Heb. 11:1). Communism, because it opposes God, is doomed to failure if only the good people of the world will allow themselves to be God's instruments, proclaiming the Gospel as man's hope, and as the summit of his dignity. Fr. Parker has seen his own national identity submerged in the artificial and manipulative program of the totalitarian state that holds the Hungarian people hostage; therefore he has a profound recognition of the spirit of the American people who have welcomed him, and he appreciates the depth of the values that should underlie true loyalty to the American nation and how necessary these values are to the defense of human dignity. "The Cross and the flag will be forever the most effective antagonist against the Hammer and the Sickle," he is fond of saying.

"For you shall see the land before you . . ." (Deut. 32:52). As for the Church, Fr. Parker sees great signs of its renewal already in his own Abbey. He ultimately hopes that St. Michael's Abbey will be able to expand its work to other parts of America, and perhaps even to international missionary activity. St. Norbert—born rich, made poor for the Gospel, and serving the Church all over Europe in his time—is a symbol of a truly universalist spirit, a spirit that Fr. Parker believes can make an important contribution to bridging the gaps between the First, Second, and Third Worlds. In time God will bring great flour-

ishing to His Church; Fr. Parker notes that the highest period of the Catholic Reformation initiated by the Council of Trent did not take place until one hundred years after the close of that Council. The renewal of the Church will take time and sacrifice, but it will come in all its fullness.

When Fr. Parker was blessed as Abbot, he chose as his motto "Succisa Virescit," referring to "that which was cut off"—namely the Abbey of St. Michael in Hungary—flourishing and growing anew as the Abbey of St. Michael in California. In this way he has himself recognized the connection between his own personal vocation and a particular religious community. Abbot Parker is a witness to the totality of commitment to religious life, in that his personal history is linked in a profoundly intimate and interior fashion to the Abbey that has received his consecration and service. His call to the priesthood was not only priestly but specifically Norbertine, and developed with the specific components of priest, teacher, and member of a prayer community. After his ordination, his priesthood was linked to the Order by his obedience to his superiors but also by the fact that his vocation was shaped by the needs of the Abbey, first as theologian and novice master, then as a leader of an exile community, then as pioneer of the new priory, creator of its particular identity and coordinator of its independence, and finally as the first head of the fully established Abbey in its new location. Abbot Parker's life is formed and shaped by the destiny of St. Michael's Abbey, and his own experience, in turn, has left an enduring mark upon its life—the mark of faithfulness, vision, hope, and courage.

VI.
Father William G. Most

Dubuque, Iowa has been called the "Rome" of the Midwest. Stretched along the Mississippi River and resting gently on the rolling hills of northeastern Iowa that rise up from the vast expanse of the heartland plain, Dubuque is a city of churches, convents, and schools whose architecture reflects the enduring contribution of Irish and German immigrants; men and women of great faith and simple devotion, often poor in the eyes of the world, but also rich in an appreciation of God's mercy and providential care—an appreciation that found its expression in their civic life.

This environment, receiving as it did the riches of the Church, was fertile ground for the development of vocations to the priesthood earlier in this century. Such vocations flourished, and with them the intellectual life that is so vital in preparing future priests for the ministry of the Gospel. It is not surprising, then, that Dubuque produced priests of keen mind and humble heart, men who saw the Universal Church with the discernment of brilliant and disciplined theologians and the faith of the simple farmers and craftsmen who nurtured them in their youth.

Discernment and faith—these are the qualities that have fashioned and nourished the priestly service of William G.

Most. A professor at Loras College in Dubuque for over 40 years, Fr. Most has made contributions to theology that have been recognized all over the world. He has published twelve books and a host of articles on topics ranging from biblical studies to Mariology to Latin grammar.

Fr. William Most: scholar, theologian, classicist, teacher—such a description shows the richness of his life, yet it fails to grasp the core, the inspiration, the motivation that underlies all his work and gives it vitality. Fr. Most is above all a man of faith; a man who has a deep and abiding sense of the generous Fatherhood of God; a man who has a keen awareness of the shape that God's generosity has taken in his own life, and who seeks to make his every action a response to the call of God.

"You are a priest forever . . ." (Heb. 5:6). God calls each man to go beyond the things of this world and to share His own life. Some, however, He calls to a special conformity to Jesus Christ, that their identity might be caught up in the obedience of Christ to the Father. The young William Most gradually became aware of this special call as he found within himself a desire that the world alone could not satisfy. Born on August 13, 1914, young William grew up surrounded by the influences of that simple faith that has left its mark so deeply on Dubuque. St. Mary's Church, built by German immigrants, was right down the block, with its tall and dignified stained-glass windows and ornate interior that suggested both the majesty and the intimacy of a God Who has made His dwelling among us. St. Mary's parish—with its parochial school—made a profound and lasting impression upon the boy, complementing a family life that was stable and filled with that basic religious sense that expresses the heart of Catholicism.

Thus William's faith grew without the clouds of misunderstanding and confusion that creep in when men forget God in their daily lives. William's childhood taught him that he could—and should—depend upon God for everything, and this attitude deepened as he grew older. He entered grade school at St. Mary's, and began to experience the challenging and affirming influence of the priests of the diocese. Through his grade school and high school years (at Columbia Academy), William learned that doctrine, discipline, and love were not conflicting things, but rather were all components of God's fatherly concern. This concern was not only taught but also lived and exemplified by the priests that formed William in school.

"Whoever believes in the Son has life eternal" (Jn. 3:36). William realized that God's concern for men reached its greatest expression in the life of Jesus Christ. In Christ God goes beyond what was strictly necessary to reconcile mankind—His wayward children—and manifests the magnificence and abundance of His love. And through Christ man is lifted up beyond all merely temporal things and becomes a child of God "by adoption." Riches, honor, even the pleasures of knowledge that correspond to man's highest natural desires, are but "straw" when compared to life in Christ Jesus—a sharing in the very life of God Himself.

The Spirit of God worked this desire in William with greater depth during his years at Columbia College. He studied Classics, and developed a lasting appreciation for the great pagan authors, especially Virgil. For a time he considered devoting his life to the study of antiquity. The Holy Spirit, however, spoke in the depths of his heart: "Do you wish to devote your life to merely human things? Man is made for greater things than this world; he is made for God!"

A passage from Scripture kept repeating itself to him: *"What does it profit a man to gain the whole world if he suffers the loss of his soul"* (Mt. 16:26). His perspective was formed and solidified. He wanted to follow Christ—to "sell all he had," all worldly interests and ambitions, which seemed so insignificant next to the light of God that was pouring into his soul.

Of course, all who are baptized in Jesus and keep His commands are "dead" to sin. But William had had a vague sense since childhood that he was called to enter still more deeply into the mystery of Christ. Christ was obedient even unto death, offering Himself completely—as Priest and Victim—to the Father. William found that he wanted to conform himself to Christ in the fullest sense, to become an instrument through which the grace and peace of Christ could flow without hindrance, through which the fatherly generosity of God could touch the world that William had known since boyhood. The Spirit enkindled this desire within him while he was still at Columbia, and by his junior year he had make his decision.

Graduation came in 1936, and the diocese of Dubuque recognized that William Most, honor graduate from the Classics department, was an exceptionally bright candidate for the priesthood. With this in mind, the new seminarian was sent to the Sulpicians in Washington, D.C. The next four years were busy ones. In addition to his studies for the priesthood at the Sulpician seminary, William also took an M.A. in Religious Studies from nearby Catholic University of America. In 1940 he returned to Iowa and on May 18 he was ordained in the Cathedral at Dubuque.

The new priest was anxious to serve the community of his home town. He had prepared himself especially for parish work; here he hoped to be like the priests he remembered from his youth—a shining example of the fatherhood of God. At this time, Fr. Most had no thoughts about becoming a college professor; teaching and the academic life were probably the last things on his mind when he became assistant at a small town parish in Peosta, Iowa after ordination.

The pastor, Fr. Drummy, was faced with a difficult task. Besides the ordinary duties of running a country parish, the church was heavily in debt, and Fr. Drummy and his parish were constantly involved in fundraising activities ranging from parish picnics to bingo to making and selling candles. Fr. Most found himself in the midst of this activity, and he plunged in with enthusiasm. The country people had a freshness and a zeal that made them a joy to serve. The new assistant was certainly needed, and before he knew it Fr. Most was running church picnics, raising money, and—of course—contributing greatly to the running of the parish. Saying Mass, hearing confessions, becoming involved and concerned with the everyday problems of people's lives—the life of parish work seemed well suited to Fr. Most and he took it for granted that things would continue this way for a long time.

"How unsearchable are the ways of God" (Rm. 11:33). Needless to say the last thing Fr. Most expected was to find himself teaching in a college classroom by Advent of that same year. As the end of the fall semester of 1940 approached at Loras (formerly Columbia) College, Msgr. Schulte, professor of Latin and Greek, suffered a heart attack. The administrators of this diocesan-run school desperately needed someone to fill in so that the students in Msgr. Schulte's classes could finish their course of study. Facing this problem, Loras remembered its brilliant and dedicated classics student of four years ago, and Fr. Most was called quite suddenly from Peosta and given temporary status on the faculty.

This status was to last for the next three years. The situation was challenging and, at times, confusing, but these years were ones of growth and unforeseen development. Fr. Most had a great love for the classical languages, but he had not done any graduate study in these areas and he had no experience teaching on an advanced level. Therefore he had to learn how to run a classroom effectively, and Fr. Most soon realized the complexities and difficulties involved with trying to communicate knowledge to students. Simply knowing the subject matter is not enough; the teacher must be sensitive to the needs of each group of students that he teaches; he must understand their capabilities and their peculiar problems.

Perhaps partly because of his own inexperience, Fr. Most began to feel a great desire to make teaching a vital component of his ministry. With this in mind, he sought further education;

from 1943-1945 he pursued a Ph.D. in Classics at Catholic University in Washington, completing all the requirements in just over two and one-half years of study. Here Fr. Most became more aware of the Fathers of the Church, and became convinced that they should have a more prominent place in the study of the classical era. The Fathers, in turn, awakened in him an interest in theology that would become more significant as his academic career progressed.

That career had now become the dominant theme of his priesthood. Fr. Most's desire to be an instrument had brought him to an influential position at the very same college where this desire had first taken shape. In 1946 he resumed his teaching position at Loras College on a permanent basis, and became immersed in the intellectual life and in pastoral ministry to students.

Concern for the students was uppermost in the mind of the new professor-priest as he attended to his duties at the College. Desiring to make the Church Fathers as accessible as possible, Fr. Most paid special attention to the particular assistance that his students needed in translating patristic texts. His efforts led him to compose a textbook edition (published in 1949) of St. Augustine's *City of God* which included translation notes specifically designed to respond to the real needs of students. His concern, however, did not stop at the classroom; he knew that being a priest meant being involved with his students as persons—embracing the whole drama of student life and serving as an instrument of God's direction in the midst of the joys, sorrows, ambitions, and difficulties of the young people entrusted to his care.

Therefore, in addition to shaping minds, Fr. Most made himself available for spiritual direction, seeing students for up to three hours a day during these early years. As he sought to draw others more deeply into the mystery of Redemption, he found that his own understanding increased, and with it his trust in God.

One of the most important aspects of this increase was his discovery of the central importance of Mary in the Redemption. For many people, the 1940's had been a sobering time, demonstrating the frightful depths to which the human heart is capable of sinking, bringing with it war and destruction, concentration camps, and a brutal and inhuman use of technology against millions of innocent people.

As the decade drew to a close, Fr. Most began to learn that there was a profound hope for this crippled humanity—that peace for mankind rested within the heart, within the faithful obedience, of the Mother of God. Our Lady of Fatima particularly spoke to people of this age, and Fr. Most began to seek a way to include her message in his direction of students. He found that the message of Fatima could not be dismissed as simply "private revelation"; the message was the Gospel itself, the Good News of salvation preached to the present era of men from a most eloquent and authoritative source.

Determining henceforth to shape his own preaching according to this message, the essence of which he found consistently in the teachings of the Church, Fr. Most consecrated his priesthood to the Immaculate Heart of Mary and set out with a renewed mission as the instrument of her who brings Christ to all.

At about this time, several students approached him and asked if he would be willing to outline a program for a study club they were forming on Mariology. He agreed, and this task enabled him to draw together all that he knew about Mary and her place in spirituality. The outlines soon developed into a book. In 1954 the first edition of *Mary in Our Life* appeared, and it brought international recognition. *Mary in Our Life* appeared in three more editions and was translated into six languages, and in 1955 it received the Marian Library Medal from Dayton University.

The book established Fr. Most's reputation as a writer who could present detailed theological topics—particularly Marian

themes—in a way that made them understandable and relevant
to all. Thus the sensitivity that characterized his teaching style
became available, through his written works, to larger groups of
people. The underlying motivation for all his work in communicating ideas was—and remains—the ministry of preaching the
Gospel. In reflecting on the priestly vocation and its presence in
his own life, Fr. Most focuses particularly on the call to preach.
The words of St. Paul, *"I came not to baptize but to preach"* (1
Cor 1:17) are not intended to downgrade the sacramental aspect
of the priesthood but rather to emphasize the presentation of
the Good News—in the whole life and example of the priest to
be sure—but particularly in *words*. These words call for faith,
or the enrichment of faith, from those who hear them.
Expressing and communicating the word of God in every
possible situation—making that "word" a salvific one in people's
lives—this became central to Fr. Most's whole mission as a
priest.

At this point, however, Fr. Most confronted his most difficult and troubling challenge, a disturbance that touched the
very heart of his presentation of the faith. He had been studying the treatises of the great theological schools, and was reflecting on their presentations of the mystery of grace and pre-
destination. One day in 1952, he was reading a commentary on
St. Thomas Aquinas by the great Dominican Reginald Garrigou-
Lagrange. The style was fluid and convincing, the thought logical and penetrating, but its implication was distressing. Père
Garrigou-Lagrange's explanation of divine providence, in its attempt to be philosophically consistent, seemed to say that God
reprobates and elects "blindly"—that is, He saves or damns
without any concern for the individual soul. How then can it be
said that God, who cannot change or be moved by anything,
really *cares* about each and every man, and if He does, how is it
that any are eternally lost? Does not God *"will that all men be
saved and come to the knowledge of the truth"* (1 Tm. 2:4)?

Sitting in his study on that day, Fr. Most wondered about the answer to the questions that he had just raised. But this answer, as mysterious as the love of God itself, eluded him. He found himself confronted with "darkness"; he believed in the mystery of God's love, and for the present that would have to be enough. It was October 11, the Feast of the Motherhood of Mary.

"Lord I believe, help my unbelief" (Mk. 9:24). For the next two years Fr. Most carried on his ministry with an attitude of trust in God based on faith. Finally out of the darkness of faith which he had experienced that day an answer began to take shape in his mind: God is our Father. He wants all His children to turn out well and be saved. He determines to reject (reprobate) only those who gravely and persistently reject His graces. All others, He determines to save (predestines) not because of their merits—which come from His goodness—nor even because of their lack of resistance to His grace, but because in the first place He wanted all to turn out well so as to save them. Therefore He saves all those who do not prevent Him by their resistance. If we are good it is totally because of His gift, but if we are evil it is totally because of our resistance to that gift; evil men do not allow their Father to make them into His children, to empower them with *"the freedom of the sons of God"* (Rm. 8:21).

This understanding leads back to faith, and to the realization that man is truly nothing without God, yet because of God's goodness he is raised to the status of sonship and given an inheritance in the Kingdom. *"Not a hair on your head shall be harmed"* (Acts 27:34). This very simple presentation of Divine providence became the theme of a major work of theology. Fr. Most composed an eighty-one page summary of his theory in Latin, and distributed it to noted theologians all over the world, requesting their comments and criticisms. Taking all of the responses—both positive and negative—into account, Fr. Most composed a lengthy and detailed treatise, which was published

in Latin in 1963. The work was critically acclaimed by many;
several theologians saw in it a key breakthrough in one of the
most difficult and most disputed areas of theology.

While the world reviewed and evaluated his scholarly en-
deavors, Fr. Most continued to attend to those who passed
through the doors of Loras College year after year. He developed a method of teaching basic Latin that involved the reading
of specially-designed texts rather than the memorization of
grammar tables. This technique tended to maintain the students'
interest and resembled more closely the manner in which they
learned their native language. Fr. Most eventually published
three textbooks of *Latin by the Natural Method* that were based
on his teaching approach.

Such was the spirit and outlook on life that characterized
Fr. William Most on the eve of the Second Vatican Council. He
had based his priesthood on a response to the call of God, on
firm faith, on total dependence upon God and His merciful
providence, on docility to the Holy Spirit. Fr. Most had built his
house upon solid rock; he had remained true to the essence of
his calling, seeking his "treasure" beyond the limits of earthly
existence even as the world gave him recognition for his
achievements. Fr. Most was prepared to receive the gifts of God
and be His instrument through which the Spirit of God could
be poured forth, manifesting God's fatherly love.

This kind of preparation was essential in discerning the
voice of the Spirit in the teachings of Vatican II, a voice too often drowned out by the confusion and turmoil that followed the
Council both in the world and in the Church. The 1960's
brought rebellion to college campuses, and the decline of moral
standards. This was accompanied by a decrease in intellectual
vigor, a loss of the "hunger" for the truth. Many in the Church
were touched by these afflictions; Fr. Most saw some of his fellow priests invoke Vatican II as a justification for ignoring the
Church's authority and for disposing of authentic spirituality,

replacing it with a "new spirituality" that rejected any form of voluntary sacrifice.

For Fr. Most this touched the very root of his response to the call of God. That response involved sacrifice at its center; he easily saw that the priesthood is folly if sacrifice has no value. Priests must give up many things if they are to serve God faithfully; this is all part of their participation in the Priesthood of Christ, which embraces the mystery of the Cross. To be a priest is to recognize that love conquers sin in the reality of God suffering on the Cross. For Fr. Most the decline in vocations that has followed the Council proceeds from this loss of the sense of the Cross. Also, the unwillingness to sacrifice means that man's horizons are limited to this world and what it has to offer. In the present day men seem bound by these limited horizons; they are unable and unwilling to rise to the challenge of Christ, and have become deaf to the Spirit of Truth. Nevertheless that Spirit continues to speak to the world, and, as long as He does, Fr. Most will continue to manifest His offering of love to men.

One of the most important aspects of his faithfulness to the Spirit is his tireless effort to affirm and proclaim the authentic teaching of the Second Vatican Council. This he has done and continues to do in books and articles, most significantly *Vatican II: Marian Council*. Published in 1972, this work presents once again the central themes of *Mary in Our Life* along with the significant developments introduced by the Council, which, Fr. Most points out, said more about the Blessed Virgin than any previous council.

Another aspect of the Council that Fr. Most addresses is the concept of the People of God. In *Covenant and Redemption* he writes of the intimate relationship between God and His people, and the obligations toward these people that God takes upon Himself by virtue of His promises and in the fullness of Jesus Christ.

In response to misrepresentations of the "spirit of the Vatican II" Fr. Most has produced works on Christology and Scripture which express the continuous and ever-vital teaching of the Church. In *The Consciousness of Christ* he defends the human knowledge of Jesus in a manner that reflects the full implication of the Word-made-flesh. At a time when many of his colleagues are advancing novel theories about Jesus Christ, His self-consciousness, and His awareness of His mission and divinity, Fr. Most presents Christ as the Incarnate Word; aware, purposeful, and filled with power. *"I lay down my life for my sheep"* (Jn. 10:15).

Some other theologians approach the revealed word of God, as expressed in Sacred Scripture, with a critical spirit that reflects a secular mentality and often a loss of faith. In *Free from all Error* Fr. Most addresses their theories—so often surrounded by an air of authority—by displaying the real and direct action of the Spirit who has given Scripture to men, along with defending the value of critical techniques—properly used—for shedding light upon the meaning and context of Scripture.

Thus Fr. Most's theological work after the Council has centered on more basic themes, as demanded by the crisis within contemporary theology. Underlying the more recent work, however, is the same evangelical theme that has informed all of Fr. Most's theology and pastoral work: God is alive and well, active in the lives of men, majestic and powerful, yet approachable by the humble and filled with overflowing love that finds its supreme expression in Jesus Christ.

Armed with this message, Fr. Most continues his work in all facets of his priestly ministry. Above all there is the continued tireless attention to his "flock," the students at Loras College. Fr. Most is now 72 years old, yet he still teaches four classes a semester ranging from the Greek philosophers to Scripture study to the Fathers of the Church. And his classes are usually filled to capacity. Fr. Most is today one of the most popular figures on the campus. Nicknamed "Ducky" in reference to his longtime position as coach of the diving team, Fr.

Most cultivates ease and rapport with his students without compromising the word he preaches, a word that often makes unpopular demands on the young people of today.

Nevertheless he always presents the truth with love. He structures his classes so that they provide the greatest benefit for students, compiling study questions and review tapes at the expense of his own time. His efforts are intended to lead students to the consideration of Christian realities, and he often uses the thought of the ancients as a springboard for the discussion of the content of revelation. In this way he hopes to focus the mind of the contemporary student, who is surrounded by the distractions of materialism, upon the profound truth of the Christian mysteries.

The communication of this truth motivates Fr. Most to continue his activity. He is convinced that his place at the college continues to be a vital component of his personal vocation as a priest. His ministry is to bear witness to a truth that might not be proclaimed to these students if he were to leave. In this way Fr. Most perceives his own role in the pervasive and loving providence of God.

It is a role that shapes his every activity. Fr. Most greets students with warmth and attentiveness in the hallways and around the campus. He takes most of his meals in the student cafeteria, listening to their difficulties and participating in their conversations—teasing them when appropriate and advising them when they seem willing to listen. In all of his interaction with students he seeks ways to communicate ideas, for all situations are ripe for the presentation of the Gospel.

Fr. Most, theologian and world-famous author, remains a priest first. As a priest he has suffered the trial of being the bearer of an unpopular and widely-ignored message. But he has endured because of his recognition of his dependence on a God who is full of goodness, and Who desires to communicate that goodness to him as an adopted son, and through him, as a priest, to others. This recognition has fostered within him an attitude of prayer, an attitude of trust in God and in the maternal direction of the Blessed Mother. And so he would be the first to affirm that his activities—whether they be scholarship, teaching, or spiritual direction—do not come from his own goodness. They come rather from the power of God that is given to him in response to prayer and for the purpose of directing himself and others to God in Jesus Christ the High Priest.

Photo by Bachrach

VII.
Father George W. Rutler

The Spirit of Truth works among all social classes, among men and women of education, laborers, businessmen, farmers, students, the unemployed, and the socially important and powerful. Beyond their particular life situations there lies a deep unity among people, grounded in their common humanity and the call that each of them receives to share the life of God in Christ Jesus. It is not surprising, then, that men who share in the ministerial priesthood of Christ should come from all walks of life. Further united by their special conformity to the Person of Christ, priests nevertheless manifest the richness of Christ and His redemptive action within the context of their own background and personal development, which brings to the ministry of each a particular character and relevance.

For Father George William Rutler this character is well defined, and the fruit of a unique collection of experiences. Fr. Rutler is an Ivy League graduate, a musician and painter, an art historian with an extensive collection, a sportsman and long distance runner, and a writer and lecturer with a considerable breadth of education and a wealth of erudition. His priesthood, however, is central to his life, and his range of interests and activities serves to mold him into an apostle who is capable of preaching the Gospel in a wide variety of situations and with a deep and penetrating knowledge of people.

Furthermore his priesthood is something that he particularly cherishes because his vocation was intimately connected to a journey of faith—a journey that brought him to full communion with the Church of Christ and to the mission of deepening and strengthening that Church.

"His love is strong, his faithfulness eternal" (Ps. 117:2). This path of the Spirit began for George Rutler in a pious Episcopalian home with devoted parents. Adolphe Rutler saw duty in the second World War as a Merchant Marine officer on convoys to Russia in the years prior to George's birth on March 23, 1945. George's childhood was filled with the familiar scenes of Anglican life; like many Episcopalian boys he sang in the church choir, and he would be in church every Sunday, sitting attentively in his choirboy's starched collar and listening to the rector preach. Perhaps someday he would preach in the same way, he often thought to himself.

When George entered school in New Jersey he had already begun to demonstrate that he had unusual intelligence. At the age of five he memorized the Gettysburg Address so that he could present it to his kindergarten teacher. As he approached high school he developed a love for the Classics, and his abilities had enabled him to skip several grades. Thus at the tender age of 12, George entered the advanced program of the public high school.

He also became more familiar with the world around him. This world included Catholics, who engaged in a variety of practices that were more or less unfamiliar to George. He remembers once entering a Catholic church as a small boy, seeing the multitude of candles, and thinking that the church was on fire!

George mainly remembers associating Catholics with certain ethnic and cultural groups. The thought that an Anglo-Saxon like himself could ever be a Catholic never entered his mind. It just wasn't something that was done. Beyond these impressions George knew very little about Catholicism; he was aware that there was "a very important and good Christian gentleman" in Rome who called himself "Pius XII." He also knew that the Catholic Church was vast, and at the time seemed to him rather "unfriendly."

Therefore when George graduated high school at the age of 16, the Catholic Church—large but foreign, and apparently irrelevant to his situation—occupied no important place in his life. His long term goal was to become an Episcopalian clergyman, a task that seemed worthy of his intelligence and his genuine zeal for God's word. In 1961 he began four years at Dartmouth, and the Ivy league atmosphere—permeated with a sophisticated skepticism—moved the young college student to react by reflecting more deeply on his religion. Modern atheistic philosophies, masking themselves as "intellectual," obviously did not provide the answers. George's French teacher was an existentialist who, after having his students read Sartre and Camus extensively, one day committed suicide. It did not seen as though truth could be found in such futility. *"The believer shall not stumble"* (Is 28:16).

Historical study, however, revealed the development of the Christian faith, and the origins of the "Anglican Communion" to which the Episcopal Church in the United States belonged. George saw that the Church of England had split from the Church of Rome in the 16th century, and he wanted to be sure that his own faith was rooted in the teaching and mission of the apostles and not the product of some confusing set of historical circumstances. This desire moved him toward a particular perspective of high Anglicanism known as "Anglo-Catholicism," that emphasized doctrine, ritual, and apostolic sense. The connection between the Church and Jesus Christ, he concluded, was of the utmost importance; *"since we have a great priest over the house of God, let us draw near with a true heart . . ."* (Heb. 10:21-22).

Meanwhile, the "Roman" Church had convoked an Ecumenical Council, an event that made no impression on George while he was in college. "High Church" Episcopalianism seemed vital in 1963, and took most of his attention. He became aware of the Oxford Movement, a trend within Anglicanism that had flourished in the 19th century. The Oxford movement had sought to restore authentic apostolic Christianity to the Church of England, and George immersed himself in the thinking of the great 19th century Anglican doctors, Keble and Pusey. One other leader of the Oxford Movement, however, seemed a bit untrustworthy. John Henry Newman was a rather disturbing fellow and George thought it best to avoid him, viewing him as "a man of nervous temperament who couldn't weather the storm and just went off and became a Roman Catholic." It seemed to George that the man whom Catholics call "Cardinal" Newman had "lost his faith."

In 1965, at the age of 20, George received his A.B. *cum laude* from Dartmouth. With a grant from the Ford Foundation he pursued graduate studies at the Johns Hopkins University, receiving an M.A.T. in 1966. Only now was he old enough to enter the General Theological Seminary in Manhattan. Covering an entire block of New York City, the GTS was like an English cloister complete with tutors from Oxford and Cambridge. At this time the GTS seemed relatively untouched by the turmoil raging in the seminaries of the Roman Church, and George received a thorough formation in an Episcopalianism styled very much after the Oxford Movement.

During his years in the seminary he spent summers in England, at Oxford University and assisting in the poor parishes of London's East End. He excelled in his studies and graduated first in his class in 1969, after which he was ordained to the Episcopalian priesthood and assigned to Rosemont, a church outside of Philadelphia.

Rosemont was an exemplar of high church Anglicanism; its 14th century Gothic style structure served a parish comprised of intellectuals and members of "Old Philadelphia" society. While a curate (a position that resembles that of associate pastor) Rev. Mr. Rutler received a doctoral fellowship to Oxford and, after a year and a half serving the parish, he had determined to go to England and finish his studies. In fact, he had already begun his dissertation on Newman, who had proven simply too troublesome to ignore.

Events, however, brought about a significant change in his plans. The rector of Rosemont left for a parish in New York, and the "Wardens and Vestrymen" of the Rosemont Parish elected George Rutler as the new rector. Believing that he was called to shepherd a flock, and upon the advice of his bishop, he gave up his doctoral fellowship and devoted himself to parish work.

Thus at the age of 26, the youngest Episcopalian rector in the United States found himself torn by a variety of ambitions, desires, and the mysterious stirrings of his heart. He enjoyed tending the needs of his suburban parish, riding a bicycle to his house calls and hospital visits. He also served as chaplain at Bryn Mawr College. The stimulating life of an Episcopalian rector seemed quite attractive, and George gave quite a bit of thought to the idea of settling down and raising a family. Marriage is an option for the Episcopal clergy, and the young clergyman was considered an eligible bachelor in Philadelphia society. He attended parties, gave lectures, and lived a pleasant life in a spacious and comfortable rectory.

By all secular standards George Rutler should have been quite satisfied. He was convinced, however, that something was missing; the fullness of the demands of the Gospel had to be met. He began to realize that much of Anglicanism took its outlook from the prevailing cultural establishment. It had remained stable for many years because of the relative stability of the society. Now, however, social and moral attitudes were changing all around, and the whole Episcopalian structure seemed to be following a path of accommodating itself to the new social perspective.

"Can a man make for himself gods? Such are no gods!" (Jer. 16:20). George Rutler was troubled in spirit. Was there so little substance behind the Anglican commitment to the Gospel? Commitment to the Gospel requires conformity to Christ as He is present and active on earth. Where could he find this presence of Christ?

The young rector found himself reading the *Apologia Pro Vita Sua* of John Henry Newman. Newman's reasons for becoming Catholic struck him and filled him with a certain uneasiness, but also a profound interest. He sought out an old seminary teacher, soon to become bishop, who advised him to stay away from that "dangerous book." But he did not take the advice; instead he read it again. "When I read Newman's *Apologia* it seemed to me that—just change the names and places, and it was rather what I was seeing around me."

"God is light; there is no darkness in him at all" (1 Jn. 1:5). The Holy Spirit was moving George Rutler to seek a full and firm foundation for his service to Christ. As this inspiration increased, his desire for a successful and amiable life in the rectory decreased. He saw himself more and more as someone called to preach the Gospel, and to embody that Gospel in his own life. He gave up the idea of marriage and joined the Oratory of the Good Shepherd, an international union of Anglican clergy who have a common rule of prayer and meet annually for a retreat in an English university or monastery. He was now prepared to dedicate himself totally to seeking God's will, and leading others to Him.

Nevertheless, he was surrounded by a spirit of capitulation. In 1976 the Anglican Communion voted to permit the ordination of women. He found himself confronted with a harsh reality: "Via Media", or "Middle Road" of Anglicanism was dying. As he watched the sand being washed away from under the edifice of the Episcopal Church, his eyes turned toward the

Church of Rome, and the Rock upon which it is built. *"Simon, son of John, do you love me"* (Jn. 21:17)? On a pilgrimage to the Holy Land, he spent a night by the Sea of Galilee thinking of those words. Objections to the primacy of the See of Peter seemed to fade in the light of the glowing witness that Peter had given, and was still giving to the integrity of the Gospel, an integrity his own Church had abandoned. "If it were wrong to have a Pope," he thought to himself, "it had to be very wrong that he should be so right."

Still he remained with his parish, convinced at the time that he could not abandon the flock entrusted to his care. After nine years, he had baptized and buried many, and there were countless friends. Soon, however, it became apparent to him that even his parish was slipping away. The Episcopal bishop had set up a collection to raise funds for a "counseling center" that was involved in promoting abortion. The young rector could not in conscience participate; it was obvious to him that abortion is the killing of innocent human life. The parish vestry, however, was willing to permit the collection to be taken; to take a stand against it would have been to violate the status quo, and that would have been most unpleasant indeed.

Meanwhile the remnants of the Oxford Movement had a voice in its century-old organization called the American Church Union. The ACU served as a national "umbrella" group for high church loyalists as well as for congregations that were splitting away from the Episcopalian structure. One important component of their efforts was the establishment of a journal called the *New Oxford Review*. Rutler became increasingly involved in the ACU and began to write for the journal, which adopted its new name at a conference held in Rosemont.

Thus in 1978, after having been elected national president of the American Church Union, he was able to resign the Rectorship at Rosemont. (Affectionate ties with Rosemont still remain, and a marker in the church commemorates the years that Fr. Rutler served there.) He was determined to "be ambitious for the higher gifts" (1 Cor. 12:31). The vision of the Gospel—the generosity and universality of the redemption of Christ—is much deeper, much more relevant, much more permanent than any superficial conformity to the standards of the day. Jesus is more radical than that; more daring and less subject to passing whim or established etiquette. "I stopped looking for what is correct," he reflects, "and began seeking what is holy."

The new president of the ACU, was convinced that the organization should consolidate all disaffected Episcopalian groups and make a collective submission to the See of Peter. The ACU, however, composed of many bishops and thousands of clergy and laity, was in disagreement about the direction of its future, and its president realized that God was calling him to make his submission alone.

It was not any easy decision to make; Rutler felt a deep sense of loyalty to the people who looked to him for leadership within the ACU He also knew, however, that the truth had called him—that "any future determination of my life's work should be measured by nothing other than its harmony with the will of the Holy Spirit."

That Spirit was now speaking in bright terms to anyone willing to listen, revealing the power and reliability of the Holy See, the guarantee of the voice of the Spirit and of the unity He ensures. A new Pope had been chosen in the fall of 1978; a man who had endured all the evils of the 20th century—atheism, fascism, communism—and who had proclaimed the Gospel in the midst of them with humility and genius. Karol Wojtyla was an inspiring choice, uniquely prepared to preach the word of God to this age with the authority of Christ. "It was quite clear that the Holy Spirit was doing something miraculous," George William Rutler recalls, "and I wanted to be a little part of it."

"In the one Spirit we were all baptized" (1 Cor. 12:13). In September of 1979 he approached Terence Cardinal Cooke, Archbishop of New York, and requested to be received in the Roman Catholic Church. Rev. Rutler did not know what would

constitute his service within the Catholic Church, or if he could even be a priest, but he knew that he wanted to be a shepherd. It had become almost an instinct for him to lead, and that instinct now manifested itself as a call to share in the priesthood of Christ, to possess a priesthood that had direct contact with the Body of Christ, immersed in and offering His sacrificial love.

On September 28, 1979, George Rutler embraced the fullness of the Christian life in union with the Body of Christ, formally entering the Catholic Church in a private ceremony at St. Patrick's Cathedral. As he awaited his first communion in the Mass that evening, he reflected upon the reading from the Old Testament appointed for that day. The prophet Haggai proclaims: *"The silver is mine, and the gold is mine, says the Lord of Hosts. The latter splendour of this house shall be greater than the former, says the Lord of Hosts; and in this place I will give prosperity, says the Lord of Hosts"* (Haggai 2:8-9).

This indeed was a familiar passage; it was the text of the first sermon he had preached at his installation as Rector in Rosemont. The call of the Holy Spirit was consistent, and assured him that all the gifts God had given him as an Anglican had not been lost; rather they had been fulfilled at last. The Church that had at once seemed so foreign was now seen as home, and he knew that nothing he had left was greater than the mystery that lay ahead of him. With this in mind, George Rutler rose from the pew and approached his Eucharistic Lord.

Cardinal Cooke was determined that his new convert should pursue the Catholic priesthood. Sent to Rome to fulfill any requirement that might stand between him and ordination, "Mr." Rutler found himself in a curious position. Living in the North American priests' residence, he watched the others say Mass and hoped for the day he could join them. Formerly he had had a staff and a large residence on Fifth Avenue; by contrast his new room in Rome had a bare lightbulb and a broken window with an obscured view. Yet this was a glimpse of the joyful detachment that brings a man close to Christ, the poverty that makes saints. *"The Son of Man has nowhere to lay his head"* (Mt. 8:20).

For two years George Rutler studied theology in Rome during which time he was ordained a deacon. Then he returned to New York to answer the call of Cardinal Cooke. This bishop, who possessed the full and authentic commission given by Christ to his apostles, stretched forth his hands and communicated that commission to Fr. Rutler. An eternal priesthood—instituted not by mere men but by God Himself—took hold in his soul. Back in Rome, he completed his doctoral studies, finishing the thesis on Newman that he had begun at Oxford. The holy Cardinal who had captured his attention, pricked his conscience, and enlightened his mind was present once again as his journey reached its summit.

Fr. Rutler returned to the United States and began his service in the Archdiocese of New York. The whole of his life experience had taught him a great deal about the challenge of Christian life and the manner in which that challenge should be presented to all kinds of people. And now he had the power of the sacramental and preaching ministry; he was the hands of Christ, reaching forth to bind the wounds of His sheep. *"I will feed them with good pasture ..."* (Ez. 34:14).

As associate pastor in Bronxville, New York he found himself very happily in a teaching position . . . with the kindergarten class of the parish school. A year later, he was assigned to Our Lady of the Victory Church near Wall Street, a church that provides the Eucharist and many hours of confessions daily for the businessmen, stockbrokers, and bankers who make up the financial district. Here Fr. Rutler, whose preaching ability began to be widely recognized, had an opportunity each day to proclaim the Good News of Salvation to some of the most influential people in the world.

Furthermore he was able to make that salvation available—to communicate its power—through the Sacrament of

Reconciliation. Fr. Rutler is convinced of the central importance of this healing ministry in the life of a priest: "a priest should never spend more time eating in any given day than he does hearing confessions." Spiritual food for others, he reasons, is more important than ordinary food for oneself.

In order to draw men to repentance—to the conversion of heart that begins and sustains one's life in Christ—they must be moved to seek the life of God. Fr. Rutler observes that many of the younger generation—who are now assuming places of importance in business and professional fields—have grown up selfish and indulged, without a sense of sacrifice and without adequate instruction in the Faith. Thus, when Fr. Rutler approaches the church pulpit he aims to break people out of the "secularism" that they have ingested during the course of their daily lives without even realizing it. When this contact has been made, he can begin to instruct, and to challenge people with the demands—and the splendor—of sanctity.

He observes that "when the new generation comes into contact with the authentic teaching and the interior life of the Church, it is a revolutionary discovery, even if they consider themselves to have been Catholic all along." This sense of discovery, which has guided and shaped his own life, also forms and directs his preaching mission.

"And men from the east and west, from north and south, will come to take their places at the feast in the kingdom of God" (Lk. 13:29). This mission above all centers on the universal vocation to holiness. Fr. Rutler sees the call to live God's life in fullness and fervor as one of the key themes of the Second Vatican Council, and the foundation of the whole renewal of the Church. The lay people must be respected as full members of the Church, truly the People of God who are called completely and without compromise to a share in the Promised Land of God's Kingdom. "Too many priests, because we are sinners, are embarrassed at telling people they have to be saints," Fr. Rutler notes. Yet the call to sanctity is the cornerstone of the dignity of

the lay person. A priest who fails to preach this message inevitably takes a patronizing attitude towards the laity.

Fr. Rutler sees this kind of attitude behind a false type of "clericalism" that infects the way many people view roles within the Church. Too often the priesthood is perceived solely in terms of a bureaucratic professionalism rather than as the task of making present the salvific ministry of Jesus. Fr. Rutler notes that when priests are considered the "professionals" of the Church, it appears as though the only worthwhile task in the service of the Gospel is priestly work. Thus in previous times lay people were not sufficiently encouraged to seize hold of their own role in the life of the Church, while in the contemporary situation some priests think that in order to involve the people in the Church they have to put them at the altar doing specifically priestly functions. Both attitudes, Fr. Rutler insists, deny the value of the unique task of the laity to evangelize the world from within.

"*. . . by one man's obedience many will be made righteous*" (Rom. 5:19). Fr. Rutler is determined to inform all of his priestly activities with that sense of the universal call to holiness, linked as it is to the universal mission of the Church of Jesus Christ. He has recently begun a university chaplaincy and now lives at St. Agnes Church on 43rd Street in Manhattan. Here he encounters a wide variety of business people as well as the whole range of society that passes through the busy life of mid-town Manhattan on any given day. The variety and richness of experience in his own life enables him to reach out to a diverse community, and his own spiritual journey has invested him with a keen insight into the mystery of the Church and its significance in the lives of everyone. "It is hardly enough to say 'I obey the Pope.' We have to be taught to love the Pope, to love the Church," he says.

This love for the Church, springing forth from a profound love for Jesus Christ, is the fruit of Fr. Rutler's search and the center of his experiences, his apostolate, his witness. From the

Ivy league and Episcopalianism to Rome and the Rock of Peter to a world that longs for the message of salvation, Fr. Rutler has followed and continues to follow the spirit of Christ; he has been summoned to embrace the unity of the Church, to foster that unity, and to deepen that unity. The holiness that Fr. Rutler seeks for himself and for the people in his care finds its source in the unity which is Christ, whose presence is the strength and the guarantee of the life of God's people.

Photo by Stegner Portraits, Inc.

VIII.
Father Rawley Myers

Pick up a newspaper or turn on the television these days and there is a good chance that you will hear something controversial about the Catholic Church. The media projects a definite image of the Church—a picture of internal dissension and confusion. In the news one often gets the impression that no one among America's Catholics really knows what to believe, or what to do.

But what is the Church really like here in the United States? Does real faith remain in the hearts and in the homes of the Catholic people, a people who are so often cited as a justification for all manner of unusual theories that, in the final analysis, tend to break down such faith? In the midst of what seems like such a confusing situation, do people still believe in the Church? Do they still trust in God?

Fr. Rawley Myers is convinced that they do. In nearly forty years as a priest of Christ, Fr. Myers has served ordinary good Catholic people from the heartland to the Rockies; hardworking family people who live lives imbued with a sense of value and direction. They are people of faith, and people whose understanding is not complicated by the disturbances of "sophisticated living." Many carry the cross of Christ in obscu-

rity yet with great heroism in their own daily lives, thus testi-
fying to the solidity of the Church's life, the life of the risen
Jesus. They are also, however, people who need guidance and
direction as they search for the will of the Father in Christ
Jesus. *"Understand, then, that the Lord, your God, is God indeed,
the faithful God who keeps his merciful covenant . . ."* (Deut. 7:9).

"I'm all for small towns," says Rawley Myers, reflecting
upon the communities he has served, and particularly the place
where he grew up. Falls City, Nebraska was everything one
would expect a small town to be in 1924, when Mervin and
Luella Myers celebrated the birth of their second son. Mervin
was a druggist, and the drug store was an absorbing occupation
for the whole family. Everyone pitched in, and the operation of
the store was a constant source of activity. "My brother says I
was born in an ice cream can," Fr. Myers recalls.

Growing up during the depression, Rawley remembers
hard times, but also the building of strong family ties. Mom and
Dad never talked about money, and consequently he and his
brother Jim never knew how poor the family really was. They
went to a very small parochial school—one that looked like a
big old barn—and worked in the drug store during their spare
time. Throughout the difficult years there was a prevailing sense
of humor in the family. "I think humor took people through the
depression," Fr. Myers observes.

During these years Rawley first thought about the beauty
and the responsibility of the priesthood. The Ursuline Sisters
who taught in the school often spoke of the priestly vocation.
Also, when the sisters would take the children into the church
during the day, Rawley remembers always seeing the pastor,
Msgr. Healy, kneeling in prayer before the Blessed Sacrament.
Prayer, he thought to himself, must be a very important thing
for a priest.

Rawley's high school was particularly small, but it provided
an atmosphere of encouragement for him. He found that, because everyone in the school was involved in all school activi-

ties, the children had more confidence in any other project they might undertake. Some of Rawley's happiest memories come from his experience as a runningback on the football team: "When you score touchdowns and have the cheerleaders standing on their heads for you, you would never think that teen years were difficult. I've never had people cheering like that for me again in my life."

While in high school, Rawley liked girls and parties as much as any other boys his age. But the depth of the Faith had begun to make its impression on him. In literature class, Sr. Bernadette introduced her students to some of the great twentieth century English Catholic writers, including G.K. Chesterton, Hilaire Belloc, and Ronald Knox. Rawley realized that the Catholic faith was more than just questions and answers in a catechism that needed to be memorized. "The great discovery," he remembers, "was that the Catholic faith is highly intelligent." *"O send forth your light and your truth; let these be my guide"* (Ps. 43:3).

This intelligence impressed Rawley, and he decided that he wanted to be a teacher. It was this motivation—the desire to express the Faith with all of its intelligence and vigor—that caused Rawley to consider the life of the priesthood.

In 1942 he was accepted by the diocese of Lincoln and began his seminary studies in Denver, Colorado. It seemed to Rawley that the seminary formation at this time was more suited to turning out seminary professors than pastors. The candidate would spend eight years in a very reserved and structured environment, immersed in detailed academic concerns and following a way of life that was highly specified; then suddenly "the day after ordination eighty-year-old women are coming to you in the parish asking you about very personal problems." It could be quite a shock; nevertheless Rawley realized that the seminary system was designed to teach virtue, patience, and penance. It instilled the sense of discipline that a parish priest absolutely must have. *"Set, O Lord, a guard over my mouth; keep watch at the door of my lips"* (Ps. 141:3).

Meanwhile Rawley found the courses in Scripture particularly dynamic and worthwhile. Fr. William Kenneally, the Scripture professor, recognized Rawley's talents and disposition, and encouraged him to become more involved with writing. Thus Rawley became editor of the seminary magazine, and began to see journalism as a vehicle for expressing the brilliance of the message of Jesus Christ.

As ordination day approached, however, Rawley began to experience some doubts. The priesthood was such a profound reality—the intimate participation in Christ as He offers Himself for the salvation of the world—that Rawley was sure that he could never be worthy of it. Of course he knew that no one is *worthy* of the priesthood except Jesus Christ. *"It is through him that you are believers in God, the God who raised him from the dead and gave him glory"* (1 Pt. 1:21). In Christ, God gives the gift of the priestly vocation to certain men. But Rawley wondered if he deserved such a gift.

Nevertheless, this gift is given through the Church; thus when ordination finally came in his home parish in Falls City in 1949, all his worries were lifted. Fr. Rawley Myers now knew for certain that he was called to be a priest.

His first assignment was as assistant pastor at St. Joseph's parish in York, Nebraska, a place that in many ways resembles his home town. Remembering the young assistant priests whose enthusiasm had always inspired him when he was a boy, Fr. Myers delved into the life of the parish school, teaching, attending football games, and being involved in the same kinds of school activities that he had loved so much when he went to high school.

These first two years, however, were not without a certain frustration. Though Nebraska Catholics are good strong family people, they are a distinct minority. Fr. Myers looked for opportunities to share the fullness of Catholic faith with the large populations of "separated brethren" that form the bulk of most midwest communities. Because of social custom, however, there were few openings for fruitful dialogue. Nebraska, he realized, has many "satisfied Protestants."

The bishop of Lincoln knew that Fr. Myers was interested in the printed word; in 1952 he decided that Fr. Myers should be prepared to take a position as an editor for the diocese. Accordingly, he sent him to work for the *Denver Catholic Register*, one of the largest syndicated Catholic newspapers in the country at that time. After a year at the *Register*, the bishop sent Fr. Myers to the Catholic University of America in Washington, D.C., and informed the chancellor that he wanted his young priest to study journalism. When told that there was no journalism department at C.U.A., the bishop said, "Have him study philosophy. Editors need philosophy."

"All wisdom is from the Lord, and it is his own for ever" (Sir 1:1). Therefore Fr. Myers found himself spending the next three years of his priesthood in the midst of the busy life of Washington, D.C. The school of Philosophy, dominated at that time by the impressive figure of Fr. Ignatius Smith, O.P., was perhaps a bit overwhelming for the unassuming Fr. Myers. "I have always admired *intelligence*, though I have very little of it myself," Fr. Myers says; indeed the scholarly stature of Fr. Smith was a great source of inspiration to him. And despite his modest assessment of himself, Fr. Myers demonstrated enough intellectual capability to earn his Ph.D. in Philosophy in 1955. He took his degree, put it in a trunk, and headed back to the farms and fields of Nebraska, to the rural people who needed his priestly care.

Upon his return he found himself heading up a new and ambitious project from the bishop, who was determined to hold a mission in every parish in the diocese over the next two years. Fr. Myers travelled to Omaha to meet with the Redemptorist Fathers—who are experts at giving missions—in order to obtain advice and direction for his own diocesan mission team. The Redemptorists told him that 150 missions in two years was impossible. "Well, impossible or not, we have to do it," Fr. Myers replied. And so they did. Fr. Myers himself preached in one third of the missions that he organized during the years of 1956 and 1957, seeking to inspire the people in each parish to conversion of heart, a sense of the presence of God, and a deeper Christian life. ". . . *you must consider yourselves dead to sin but alive for God in Christ Jesus*" (Rom. 6:11).

After the missions were completed, Fr. Myers received a temporary assignment to administer a small town parish. This task, as it turned out, lasted fourteen months, and it gave Fr. Myers a different perspective on the work of parish priests, especially country priests. He found the experience to be a very lonely one, and it gave him a deeper understanding of the basic struggles that many priests in obscure places must face within themselves. Fr. Myers remembers that, during the late 1950's, parish facilities all over America were undergoing rapid development—new buildings, new schools, and renovations. Perhaps this exterior work represented some of the frustration and loneliness that parish priests felt. "A lot of priests were builders because they were bored," he reflects. Nevertheless Fr. Myers did not build; he simply attended to his duties in the parish and waited.

Finally, a permanent pastor was found, and Fr. Myers was able to move on. In 1958 he became assistant editor of the Lincoln diocesan newspaper and, one year later, editor, a position he would hold for nine years. During this time he was also one of the chaplains of the Newman Center at the University of Nebraska (1958-1962), chaplain of the diocesan convent (1963-1967), and an instructor in the CCD teacher training program, which went from parish to parish teaching religion teachers.

One would think that the editor of a diocesan newspaper would have a great deal to say about the events that were happening in Rome during the Second Vatican Council. Nevertheless, although there were regular reports in the paper on the sessions of the Council, Fr. Myers dedicated himself primarily to local events and diocesan activities.

It was not until after the close of the Council that things began to change in Nebraska, and initially Fr. Myers greeted this trend with enthusiasm. The renewal of the Church—and the greater sense of the community life of God's People that it hoped to foster—seemed to be a promising thing, and Fr. Myers was anxious to be involved in it. With this in mind, he took on the pastorate of the parish in York—the same one in which he had first served seventeen years earlier. *"The soil has given its harvest, God, our God, has blessed us"* (Ps. 67:6).

This interval as a pastor lasted two years. These years were particularly difficult ones for the Church in the United States; an attitude of curious and unfounded innovation was sweeping through churches all over the country; it was a mentality that had little to do with what the Spirit of God had called for at the Council. Fr. Myers realized this, but he also knew the character of his own people. "Farmers aren't going to change very fast," he thought to himself.

At this time, Fr. Myers still had a long-standing desire to be a teacher, and when a position opened at Kennedy College for a philosophy lecturer, he saw his opportunity. Thus, after a year of supplementary study at the University of Notre Dame, he joined the faculty at Kennedy, where he taught Introduction to Philosophy, Ethics, and History of Philosophy. Kennedy was a secular college, and Fr. Myers saw here a chance to expose his students to a glimpse of the intellectual heritage that had developed around a foundation of faith in Jesus Christ. Fr. Myers found that many students, Catholic and non-Catholic, lacked an intellectual formation in religion. This discovery continues to cause him distress to the present day. "Ninety per cent of the kids I know have not read one Catholic book," he laments, remembering the impact of clear and confident writers like G.K. Chesterton on his own youth, authors who still hold the most prominent place in his library. *"Teach me the demands of your precepts"* (Ps. 119:39).

After three years at Kennedy College, Fr. Myers began to experience more serious problems with the arthritis that had long afflicted him. However, when he spent some time helping out in a parish in Colorado Springs, Colorado, he found that the high altitude and dry air significantly improved his condition. Therefore, after twenty-one years of priestly ministry in the diocese of Lincoln—years that were characterized by variety of service yet consistency of dedication—he applied for a transfer to the diocese of Denver.

In 1972, Fr. Myers came to Colorado Springs permanently, as associate pastor of St. Mary's Church. During these years in Colorado, though he devoted himself primarily to pastoral work, he did not by any means neglect his writing. Fr. Myers wrote extensively, drawing from the whole of his experience, and produced several books, most notably the critically acclaimed *Journal of a Parish Priest*. He also became a regular contributor to periodical publications, including Fr. Baker's *Homiletic and Pastoral Review*.

As the *Journal* suggests, however, the parish continued to be central to his ministry. In Colorado, Fr. Myers found himself under a new bishop and in the service of another local manifestation of the Universal Church. That universality was—and still is—apparent to him not only because his church is joined to Christ, but also because of the witness of its people, a testimony that convinces Fr. Myers continually that many of the faithful—whatever contrary reports might say—are truly close to the Lord and aware of the unity of His Body.

This unity involves continuity with all that is perennially valid. In his fourteen years in Colorado Springs, as well as in all his previous service, Fr. Myers has observed that sense of continuity in the faithful, and their love of the Faith. "So much of what the daily papers say about the Church is the idea of the editor," he notes, commenting on the media-created notion that the very core of the Church is in a state of upheaval. He recognizes the fact that the common people, and even some of his fellow parish priests, may be too complacent; and others are all for the implementation of fashionable human trends in parish life, trends that obscure the reality of the Gospel. He does not, however, feel that radical innovations—so often undertaken in the name of "the people"—are truly what real flesh and blood Christian men and women need or want. He comments on the self-appointed experts "who think they know what's best for the people: I wish they'd talk to the people sometimes." *"Let the congregation of the faithful sing his praise!"* (Ps. 149:1).

These people, Fr. Myers consistently finds, want the sense of the beauty of their faith to be preserved; they seek leadership in living a Christian life—a life founded and sustained by the sacraments; and they want encouragement and guidance in the difficulties of their daily lives. Fr. Myers notes that life has become more difficult for many people because of the confusion of modern society and—an added dimension he has discovered since coming to Colorado Springs—because of the problems of city life. Cities have made life hard for low-income families who feel "cooped up" in a congested urban environment and constantly threatened by high rates of crime.

For the past four years Fr. Myers has been at St. Joseph's parish. About half of this parish is Hispanic, and there are many young families who go to church every Sunday. "We don't have scholars. We just have people who are fighting every day in the struggle for existence." This struggle includes facing certain fears that are built into contemporary life; many people are afraid to go out at night, and parents are afraid to send their children out to play. It also includes moral problems; Fr. Myers is used to hearing that "the kid is on dope or the daughter is getting married outside the Church." Often these trials are occasions that manifest God's power in suffering: "I'm just amazed at what saints we have who are parents."

"*And he took pity on them, because they were like sheep without a shepherd . . .*" (Mk. 6:34). Fr. Myers also recognizes the particular struggles of elderly people. He gives regular retreats for the elderly, and he publishes a monthly magazine of inspiration called *Star* for senior citizens or anyone else seeking encouragement. "Old people are very confused about the Church today," he notes, "and they built these churches and they have a right to a little peace and happiness." Fr. Myers finds that a great deal of the work with the elderly simply involves reassuring them that God has not forgotten His people—"telling them that the Church isn't falling to pieces."

By contrast, young people are greatly influenced by the secular world around them. The message of conversion always needs to be preached, but it is difficult to get teenagers to involve themselves in Church life, or even to attend Mass regularly: "They go when they feel like it. That's the new spirit." Fr. Myers observes that young people often have not yet come to understand that they owe *gratitude* to God.

Indeed, it is the sense of the presence of God and responsiveness to His love that will determine the vitality of the Church in the future. What is important is not so much better organizational strategies or pastoral programs but rather a better relationship with God. "One prayer," Fr. Myers says with a grin, "is worth more than ten meetings." Prayer is a fundamental, yet often elusive, aspect of being a Christian. Fr. Myers observes that we will talk about prayer, theorize about it, even invent new ways to pray . . . as long as we don't have to do it. "There are a lot of games people play in religion," he says, "we will do anything not to pray."

Why don't we pray more? In some sense it is because prayer is linked to the Cross of Jesus. " '*Are you not the Christ? . . . save yourself and us as well*' " (Lk. 23:39). This was the bad thief's scornful shout at Jesus as they both hung from the cross. Perhaps at times our attitude resembles his; we do not want the cross that prayer often proves to be. Fr. Myers puts it bluntly:

prayer is often boring and difficult. "I'd rather dig a ditch from here to Chicago than pray," he says, "its easier." Nevertheless we must pray, and this means we must do more than what Fr. Myers calls "the firehouse approach," namely praying only when we are in trouble and need God to help us out.

He insists that we need a rich and full prayer life. This means that prayer of praise and glory to God is of fundamental importance. We should seek prayer of meditation, an important aspect of which is contained in the reading of the Gospels. Also of particular significance is the Rosary, which is sometimes most effective when its power is least felt. When we say the Rosary and meditate upon the mysteries of our redemption, he points out, we know that our prayer is real.

This last observation points to a particular character of Fr. Myers' priesthood—his devotion to Mary. When he was ordained, he dedicated the service of his priesthood to the Virgin Mother of God, *"because He has looked upon His lowly handmaid"* (Lk. 1:48). Fr. Myers is convinced that "she has gotten me through everything." In the spirit of Mary, Fr. Myers seeks to attend to his duties in prayer. In addition to his Mass and whatever public devotions the church is sponsoring, he sets aside an hour each day for personal prayer. As a priest, he also recognizes his specific role as a leader of prayer, both the prayer of the parish community and—by way of direction and inspiration—the prayer-lives of his people. Fr. Myers always refers to the striking yet simple example of Msgr. Healy, the pastor of his boyhood parish; the witness to prayer of this holy priest served as a model to his parishioners, including young Rawley Myers.

Thanks to Msgr. Healy, Fr. Myers recognizes the unique value of prayer before the Eucharistic Presence of Jesus. Nevertheless he recognizes that it is difficult for many of his people—busy as they are with work and raising their families—to come to the church every day. "If you can't go to the church where Christ is, invite Christ to your home," he advises. The presence of Christ and the power of his salvation, Fr. Myers knows, will always restore and strengthen God's people in firmness of faith. For this Christ will not let anyone down: "Persevering in prayer is really the answer to everything."

"It will be clear that you are standing firm in unity of spirit and exerting yourselves with one accord for the faith of the gospel" (Phil. 2:27). Fr. Rawley Myers seeks only to serve the faithful of Christ, to look after their needs and to defend their integrity. As the title of one of his books suggests, "Jesus is here," always willing to embrace his people with His redeeming love and waiting only to be called upon. Jesus is hidden, but His power is accessible, and that power is the bond that unites the Catholic people; a bond that has a strength unseen by those who do not seek the light. It is the strength of the Church, the strength of its people, the strength of their Faith—a Faith that shall not fail.

Photo by George C. Hight

IX.
Father Douglas McNeill

An old woman carefully sweeps the dirt floor inside the single room hut that shelters her family. A pot simmers gently on a wood stove in the corner, and smoke rises to touch the thatched roof. As the woman calls outside to her granddaughter, in a language that few people have ever heard, a rooster flaps its wings, and a few scraggly dogs run freely among a small cluster of four or five huts. They look almost as hungry as the people.

Every few miles there is another group of small wooden dwellings; most are only a little larger than tool sheds. Narrow dirt paths cut across dry stretches of land with sparse vegetation, and the nearest paved road is nowhere in sight. There is no electricity, no running water, and no modern sanitation. One is not surprised that this place is mission territory, and that the needs of these isolated people are a particular concern for Christ's Church. What is surprising, however, is that this place is *America*; that the kind of life one automatically associates with the "Third World" is lived here in the midst of the sloping and colorful majesty of Northern New Mexico, in the shadow of the great Rocky Mountains that loom on the horizon.

The Navajo Reservation unites over 200,000 Indians in New Mexico, Arizona, and Utah, covering a stretch of land

larger than most Eastern states. It is also—by federal defini-
tion—the poorest rural area in the nation. In this poverty stands
the hungry Christ, the homeless Christ, and the abandoned
Christ. The diocese of Gallup, New Mexico has no intention of
ignoring the suffering of Jesus; on the contrary it has established
missions for the assistance of the Indians, missions which in their
service to the poor embody the poverty of spirit which Christ
wills for His Church.

St. Bonaventure's is one such mission. Its staff of lay volunteers make it uniquely suited to the wide variety of projects
that must be carried out on behalf of the Indian people. One
man, however, stands as the focal point of the mission, and as
the source of the spiritual formation that inspires every work.

"Go and make disciples of all nations" (Mt. 28:19). Fr. Doug
McNeill is a priest with a special call to evangelization; St.
Bonaventure's parish has only twenty Catholic families, but its
territory covers the whole area around Thoreau, New Mexico,
touching the remnant of the Navajo nation and ministering to
the often desperate needs of the Navajo people, most significantly their profound need to encounter their Lord and Savior
Jesus Christ, who is yet unknown to most of them.

New Mexico, however, was the last place in the world
Doug McNeill ever expected to spend his adult life. Born in
Brooklyn to Irish immigrant parents on March 6, 1942, Doug
grew up in surroundings that differed greatly from the ones in
which he now works. Yet as a child he experienced a poverty
not unlike that which he encounters today. The McNeill's had
seven children, but Doug's father was an alcoholic and was unable to support the family. His mother worked nights as a
cleaning woman, watched the children during the day, and often
scolded her husband who came home drunk almost every afternoon.

Yet it was not a difficult house to live in. Mother set a
strong example, and Father was not in any way violent or abu-
sive. Doug remembers eating stale buns and tea for breakfast as

a child, then being sent off to school in a bright and clean uniform. Most of Doug's teachers were Xaverian brothers, and they communicated an awareness of God that made a very strong impression on the boy. *"The heavens are yours and the earth is yours"* (Ps. 89:11).

This awareness, however, did not stop Doug from getting into mischief. He and his friends were always plotting to run away from home and become "independent." Often they stole items from stores, things that they would need once they were "on their own." One night they broke into a friend's house and the father, not realizing that the intruders were children, chased them out furiously and threw a knife at the front door that barely missed Doug's head as he was fleeing the house. *"The man who fears the Lord will accept his correction"* (Sir. 32:14).

For all of their troublesome behavior, however, the boys always knew that they had done wrong and encouraged one another to go to confession. As Doug grew older he became a more responsible and more successful student, finally earning a scholarship to the Christian Brothers' high school, LaSalle Academy.

During this whole period the idea of becoming a priest had begun to take shape in his mind. Indeed it had been present since childhood, but his first inclination had been to dismiss the idea; a mischievous boy like himself, he thought, would never be worthy of the priesthood. At LaSalle, however, he received much more encouragement, and at the advice of one of his teachers he wrote to various religious orders and congregations for information.

In this way he first heard of the Missionaries of the Sacred Heart, and deep within his own heart he perceived a call to bring the message of salvation to the far corners of the world. There was something dramatic and necessary about missionary work, something that seemed to complement the desire for the priesthood that he felt so strongly.

"And he got up and followed him" (Mt. 9:9). Thus at the age of 16, Doug McNeill desired once again to leave home, but this time for a much different reason. Sacred Heart Mission Seminary in Illinois offered him the opportunity to finish his high school years in an atmosphere that corresponded to his newly found sense of direction. At this time the missionary vocation appeared as the pearl of great price, and Doug was willing to abandon the final two years of his scholarship at LaSalle in order to seek it.

Thus in the fall of 1958, Doug began nine years of association with the Missionaries of the Sacred Heart. After high school and two years of college, he made a full year novitiate in Youngstown, Ohio, where he developed a greater sense of God as the source of his vocation, and the sense that the priesthood was a particular path to holiness upon which he was called to walk, and not simply a "service in the world."

After novitiate in 1962, when Doug first formally entered religious life, he did not imagine the changes that would take place in the world during the next five years, nor the particular questions and problems that would arise regarding the way of life he had chosen. His years of preparation for the priesthood, however, passed right through the heart of these most difficult years. Doug was being prepared to be a foreign missionary in Papua, New Guinea, some 5,000 miles across the Pacific ocean. Yet with each year he became increasingly convinced that he was being called instead to the service of his native land. It seemed that there was a great deal of missionary work needed in America itself, particularly during the troubled era of the late 1960's. During the summer of 1966, Doug and several other seminarians assisted in a census of a black parish in inner city Detroit. They arrived at the rectory on their first day and found themselves in the middle of a severe incident of racial unrest so characteristic of the tension and danger that plagued the city all that summer. That afternoon, Doug spent nearly an hour under a table as bullets crashed through the rectory window and whizzed overhead.

Peace was eventually restored, and in the course of taking the census Doug confronted countless poor black families who were anxious to place their children in Catholic schools, aware as they were that Catholic schools had a tradition of educational excellence and character-building. He realized all the more the vitality of Catholic educational institutions, and the necessity of preserving them. *"Teach them to observe all the commands I gave you"* (Mt. 28:20)

Meanwhile Doug was becoming increasingly convinced that his vocation lay outside the religious life. He wrote to the vocations director of his home diocese of Brooklyn, who suggested that he pray and wait before making any decision. And so he prayed and waited. After a year he decided to write to his superiors in Rome and request secular status, and a dispensation was granted by the Congregation for Religious in the summer of 1967. With three years of theology already completed, Doug was now free to pursue the diocesan priesthood.

After leaving the structured direction of religious life, however, Doug found himself confronted with confusion about the whole of his vocation to the priesthood. In fact, he was quite sure at first that he was not, after all, called to be a priest. So he got a job as a construction worker and began seeking more permanent employment in New York City. He interviewed with the Boy Scouts and the Red Cross and made up his mind that—in any case—he definitely wanted to live a life of service.

Beyond this desire, however, there was only darkness about the future, a future that had at once seemed so settled. Yet it was a darkness of faith; Doug did not pause for a moment in the practice of his spirituality, a discipline that he had learned so well in his formation thus far. And the Holy Spirit, who had placed within him the desire to be priest and missionary, had not forgotten him or the vocation that still held promise; a vocation that would blossom anew in the midst of

Doug's own uncertainty. For *"whoever believes in me need not stay in the dark anymore"* (Jn. 12:46).

Towards the end of the summer he visited the family of his friend and former classmate Phil DeRea. It was Phil who encouraged him not to give up on the priesthood; there were a variety of dioceses in the United States "with a missionary flavor" that perhaps could use someone with Doug's training, orientation and desire to serve. As Doug thought about this possibility, one diocese in particular came to mind as a "mission diocese." Doug probably did not even know where Gallup, New Mexico was on a map, but he wrote to this large and sparsely populated diocese and explained his situation. "The vocations director must have been waiting at the Post Office," he recalls. The answer came back immediately: report to Immaculate Conception Seminary in Conception, Missouri. "So I did."

Once he had determined to resume priestly studies, Doug discovered a newfound zeal and a deep desire to be ordained into a share in Christ's eternal High Priesthood. The Spirit nevertheless was determined to test the purity of Doug's desire by requiring him to be patient. He finished his final year of theology in 1968 and expected to be ordained soon afterward. The seminary, however, would not issue a letter of recommendation to his diocese because he had not met the minimum two-year residency requirement. Bernard Espelage, O.F.M., who was the founding bishop of Gallup, would not ordain Doug without a letter from his seminary; instead he sent him to work as an assistant to the priests of a parish in Winslow, Arizona.

"Be patient, brothers, until the Lord's coming" (Jas. 5:7). During a year in Winslow, Doug assisted in teaching, organizing, and building up the parish grounds. His status was uncertain during this whole time; he had not yet been ordained a deacon and the bishop, who was retiring, had determined to leave the resolution of his status to his successor. So Doug waited in the midst of a good deal of anxiety, but also with a deeper sense of peace. He was convinced by this time that God indeed had a

plan for him, and that this period of waiting was designed to lead him to complete resignation to God's will. Meanwhile the priests were very encouraging and supportive, and the people of Winslow treated him like one of their own.

In January of 1970 the new bishop, Jerome Hastrich, was installed and immediately contacted Doug. The Bishop invited Doug on a pilgrimage to the Shrine of Our Lady of Guadalupe in Mexico, where they could get to know one another and also pray about Doug's future. At the Shrine Doug was profoundly moved by the great faith of the Mexican Indians, which brought to mind the many Indians who still waited to hear the Gospel message.

Upon their return, the Bishop quickly scheduled ordination dates for Doug, and on May 30, 1970 he was called to the priesthood. It was a day of joyful celebration in Winslow as their "adopted son," who had worked side by side with the parishioners, now approached the altar of God.

"... all our qualifications come from God" (2 Cor 3:5). Doug McNeill brought faith and patience to the service of the priesthood. The unusual and often difficult circumstances which attended the development of his vocation had given him a sense that the Holy Spirit was present and active in directing his life according to the wisdom of God. Now he was prepared to embrace his ministry with this same spirit of trust.

For Fr. McNeill this ministry would be expressed in the preaching and teaching of the faith, in the fundamental work of catechesis linked to the whole vision of Catholic education. After a year at Our Lady of Guadalupe in Holbrook, Arizona, where among other things he worked to establish the first diocesan marriage tribunal, Fr. McNeill was granted a scholarship from the Extension Society for the Home Missions to study Religious Education at Fordham University in New York. After two years—during which he was able to live at home in Brooklyn—Fr. McNeill received his M. S. degree and returned to Holbrook, where he set about establishing a religious education office for the Arizona side of the Gallup diocese.

During two years of study, Fr. McNeill had encountered many contemporary approaches to religious education and had seen their basic inadequacies. Some of the programs simply did not *teach* anything, or else they taught a vague "gospel" of earthly social responsibility rather than a Gospel centered on the power and truth of Jesus Christ. His own catechetical program, he was convinced, must proclaim the Good News of salvation. This proclamation should include the pervasive presence of Scripture understood in its fully Catholic significance. "There is power in God's Word," he often reflected, "the power to change lives."

At this time Fr. McNeill was working almost exclusively with the small Catholic population of the diocese. The vast Navajo nation, though it surrounded most of the areas in which he worked, had not yet taken a central place within his ministry; in fact he was still not fully conscious of the plight of the Indians who lived so near.

However, in 1974 things began to change. Fr. McNeill moved to the parish of St. Bonaventure in Thoreau, New Mexico where he hoped to establish the New Mexico office for religious education in the diocese. St. Bonaventure's is a "mission parish" in a community with almost no Catholics that borders the reservation. Though he was pastor, Fr. McNeill did not anticipate that the work of the parish would make many demands on him; this made it appear to be the ideal residence from which he could organize the religious education program.

A religious sister and a few volunteers comprised his initial staff, and the program was soon underway. Fr. McNeill could not help noticing the Indians who were his neighbors, but it was two years before he became actively involved with them. The gateway to full-time Indian mission work was the Southwest Indian Foundation, a diocesan social help organization that was heavily into debt. A new director was needed, and no one in the diocese really wanted to take on the task. Fr. McNeill found himself volunteering, and he was suddenly thrust headlong into the plight of the Navajo.

For many this plight is a desperate poverty and a crippling sense of helplessness. The Navajo had been a nomadic tribe, wandering the Southwest with their herds of sheep, before their confinement to a reservation a century ago. They survived a change of living habits and remain today the largest Indian tribe in the United States. But they are a people afflicted by illiteracy, unemployment on a grand scale, high infant mortality, a suicide rate that is ten times higher than the national average, rampant alcoholism, and a variety of other health problems. Hepatitis and tuberculosis are present, and—virtually unheard of in our "modern" era—there is the consistent occurrence of bubonic plague, with about four or five cases discovered each year.

Fr. McNeill began to restructure the Southwest Indian Foundation, attempting to restore a budget that was $700,000.00 in the red, and give to the organization on overall sense of purpose and direction. In the process God began to send volunteers to help him in the most needed work. *"It is to the glory of my Father that you should bear much fruit"* (Jn 14:8).

A truck driver offered his services to the mission, and he and Fr. McNeill established a route for the delivery of fresh water. With the aid of four-wheel drive vehicles the mission began bringing water to the Indians who dwelled in otherwise inaccessible places. Here Fr. McNeill became aware of other needs—the buildings in which the Indians lived were falling apart; some, in fact, had become quite dangerous. So they put their slim resources into building repair. The mission was able to build an eight-sided one room traditional Indian "hogan" for under $2000.00. Furthermore, contact with the Indians brought a greater awareness of medical and nutritional problems. Soon a nurse arrived at St. Bonaventure's as a full time volunteer, and a meals-on-wheels program was established. In order to foster greater outreach to the Indian children, Fr. McNeill began a summer camp, which also became a source of new mission workers, as some volunteer counselors got a sample of the life of the Mission and decided to stay.

Soon Fr. McNeill had a regular staff of volunteers who lived in several trailers and a house across the road from the church. The church at that time was a one-room building, part of which also served as a rollerskating rink. When one day a small Navajo boy asked him, "How come you skate in your church?", Fr. McNeill realized that the effort to communicate the reality of Christ to the Indians required a worthy roof over the real presence of Christ, and over the Eucharistic Sacrifice in which He redeems the world.

Therefore he decided to build a separate church. However, there was clearly not enough money for the kind of building he wanted. Fr. McNeill managed to raise some through donations, and the Extension Society gave $10,000. Still, he needed to finance the labor and the expertise that would be needed to put up the building. "What did I think was going to happen to let us build that church without any money?" Fr. McNeill wonders. But God made something happen. A new volunteer arrived at the mission, a man who also was an expert carpenter, plumber, and electrician. Thus the organization and skilled labor for the church was free of charge, and the community was able to erect the building in 1976 for less than $50,000.

St. Bonaventure had indeed become a demanding assignment, but also one that was beginning to bear fruit. With this in mind Fr. McNeill resigned as director of the Southwest Indian Foundation and began to devote himself exclusively to the Mission and the community that was growing up around it. He began with a conviction that had its roots in his whole previous formation and was consistent with the work he had done thus far in the service of the Church: St. Bonaventure's needed a school!

"See that you never despise any of these little ones . . ." (Mt.
18:10). Three years earlier Fr. McNeill had begun a pre-school
and he had come to realize some of the particular problems that
Navajo children face. Many of them do not receive a proper
education; often cultural and religious customs in Navajo families discourage education or any social assistance that tends to
lead Indians away from the reservation. The state government
provides boarding schools, but they do not provide the saving
truth of Jesus Christ. Fr. McNeill began to see evangelization as
the cornerstone of a beneficial education for the Navajo youth,
and the key to reaching the whole people: "Knowing Christ and
knowing their native culture and religion, they would be a
bridge in making a Navajo Catholic American," he thought.

*"Don't let your hearts be troubled. Trust in God still, and trust
in me,"* (Jn. 14:1). Fr. McNeill was convinced that God willed the
mission to provide an education centered on the Gospel. Armed
with this confidence, he did all the preliminary work in the
spring and summer of 1981 that would be necessary for St.
Bonaventure Academy to begin instruction in the fall. Only two
problems remained: he had no teachers and no school building.
With faith, Fr. McNeill forged ahead, signing on 20 children for
the fall semester—the Holy Spirit would see to the teachers, he
was convinced.

Two weeks before the school was scheduled to open, three
volunteers arrived at the Mission. They wanted to teach. Fr.
McNeill was not surprised. By putting different groups of children into different corners of the main hall next to the church,
he was able to open the school on schedule. St. Bonaventure
Academy, Fr. McNeill is convinced, was God's project rather
than his own: "He sets these things up and I trust Him all the
time, and then when I think it's all lost he pulls it all out and
says, 'see I had it all planned.' " *"Do not give up if trials come;
and keep on praying"* (Rom. 12:12).

After the first year it became obvious that St. Bonaventure
Academy needed its own school building. The Mission had a

mailing list of only 800 people—not a very large resource from which to raise funds. Continuing his trust in God, however, Fr. McNeill sent out a letter in which he explained the situation of the Academy. One woman on the list had recently lost her daughter in a car accident, and had received an out-of-court monetary settlement. Though it was a large sum, she had no desire to use it personally. When she read Fr. McNeill's letter, she "heard God's voice" telling her of a worthwhile way to honor her daughter Teresa, who had a great love for children. Thus Fr. McNeill suddenly found himself with $100,000.00 for his project, and he was able to build St. Teresa Hall.

Soon more volunteers arrived at the school to teach, and others were hired to assist in its administration. The Academy purchased a number of four-wheel drive school buses so that children could be picked up and dropped off each day at the reservation; this meant that St. Bonaventure's would be one of the few Indian schools that is not a boarding school. Nevertheless, in 1984 the Mission opened a boys' group home and a girls' group home for children who come from difficult home situations. The residents attend St. Bonaventure Academy; they also have scripture study at the group home and they are brought to Mass every Sunday.

Evangelization is the key to the work of St. Bonaventure Mission; nevertheless the profession of Christianity is not required in order to receive help from the mission. Fr. McNeill wants to avoid superficial "conversions" that proceed solely from a desire for material advancement. "We're not selling Christ as a pastry," he says, "it's got to be commitment." *"Do not let your love be a pretense, but sincerely prefer good to evil"* (Rom. 12:9).

He realizes, however, that it will take a great deal of work to build the sense of commitment. Fr. McNeill expects that it will take three generations for a truly vibrant Navajo Catholic community, fully aware of its faith, to grow up around St. Bonaventure's. At this time there are almost no Navajo Catholics, yet Fr. McNeill is completely dedicated to the proposition that only Jesus Christ can raise up the Navajo people, not only to life in the Spirit but also to a dignified and truly human life on earth, one that completes their own particular talents and creative energy.

Today St. Bonaventure's Mission is thriving, with its school, pre-school, summer camp, group homes, meals-on-wheels, water delivery system, thrift shop, daily free lunch for the poor, library, and building repair service. In addition it cooperates with several state and federally funded projects—the much-needed alcoholism program and a basic medical clinic which has a doctor on duty from 10 AM to 2 PM each day (the nearest full time medical facility is 30 miles away).

Also there are several programs that have just gotten underway. In October of 1986, Fr. McNeill opened a Vocational Training School that offers auto mechanics, home repair, computers, welding, and printing. The school has been made possible by several significant contributions, including the donation of an entire print shop.

Recently the Philips Petroleum Company, after a failed mining venture in the area, donated a large stretch of property to the Mission including a mobile home development and a park for recreational vehicles. With the mobile homes, Fr. McNeill has opened a Catholic retirement center, where senior citizens can settle permanently and volunteer their many talents and services to the Mission.

Fr. McNeill also has long term goals. He hopes someday to establish a Navajo Studies Center and perhaps a college. He also hopes to have a full high school, not just for Navajo but for everyone in the diocese—at present there is no Catholic high school in the Gallup area. These goals, along with all the present work, primarily depend on private donations, which can be sent—along with any inquiries—to St. Bonaventure Church, P.O. Box 610, Thoreau, NM 87323.

Currently, the Mission confronts its tasks with a full time staff of 22. These people are not simply "volunteers" who take time out from their various busy schedules to lend a hand. Rather they are committed lay missionaries who live in the area or in the modest complex of trailers that sit across from the church on the mission grounds. Most significantly, as residents, they make up an important part of the parish of St. Bonaventure, united in Christ and in the Eucharist.

This is where Fr. McNeill sees his own place in the work of the Mission. He has a unique role as the spearhead and point of unity for all the lay workers. He offers Mass, leads prayer, and provides the formation that constitutes the soul of missionary work. In particular, by his ministry of the Eucharist, Fr. McNeill binds the whole Mission together in Christ and offers Christ, with the work of the Mission, to the Father each day. The Daily Mass, Fr. McNeill frequently stresses, is the most significant event in the life of his Mission community, and the source of its strength.

"Everything is possible for anyone who has faith" (Mk. 9:24). In this sense Fr. McNeill views himself as an "enabler," putting down the roots out of which grow all the work. These roots, above all, draw nourishment from the Church. Because of Fr. McNeill's presence, St. Bonaventure's is more than just a collection of people with good will. "The Church certifies and guarantees that our mission is truly from Christ," he insists, and he notes that his own position manifests the connection of the Mission to the bishop of Gallup and the Universal Church. Thus the mission effort is linked to the work of the Catholic Church, the work of Jesus Christ.

This Universal Church is the source of inspiration and direction for Fr. McNeill and his community. The voice of the Holy Father is authoritative, and there is no room at St. Bonaventure's for those who are not responsive to the Holy Spirit as He speaks through the Vicar of Christ. "We have had people of that kind of a mind before, and I have sent them away," says Fr. McNeill.

In the many services they provide an overall spirit of dedication to the Gospel is central. The Navajo Indians hunger not only for bread and for a better life, but also for the Word of God. Thus, in addition to the work of presenting the Catholic faith, Fr. McNeill seeks to have every activity—indeed the mission community itself—stand as an evangelical witness so that the Navajo people might know the love of Jesus. "We're trying to live Catholic social teaching in its fullness," Fr. McNeill notes, pointing out that such a commitment rules out any kind of ideological "sell-out" for the sake of quick results or purely materialistic solutions. Those who run after the radical ideologies of this world as the only vehicle for social change have no place in the work of this Mission. Fr. McNeill notes that ideologues in Christian disguise "have given up on the efficacy of the power of Christ, of the Church, of the sacraments, and we haven't done that. Why would I give up on Christ? Who else has words of eternal life?" ". . . and we believe; we know that you are the Holy One of God" (Jn. 6:69).

Thus St. Bonaventure Indian Mission continues to flourish, and Fr. McNeill's priesthood plays an integral formative and unitive role. The Mission has meant for him an opportunity to serve Christ in the poor and to teach the redeeming message of Christ. In this way the wisdom of God becomes more apparent. For indeed, the Spirit was determined that Fr. McNeill become an American missionary. As Fr. McNeill learned, it is God who is truly in charge of his life, and he has brought this attitude to his ministry. In this way the Divine plan encompasses a call to the Indian people of New Mexico to embrace redemption in Christ Jesus—a call that Fr. McNeill and the Mission seek to embody and to express.

X.
Father John Hardon, S.J.

In order to follow Jesus Christ, and to embrace the whole reality of the message of salvation, the believer must be attentive to the voice of Christ teaching, ruling, and sanctifying in a singular fashion through the office of Peter, the apostle to whom He gave the unique and universal commission: *"Feed my sheep"* (John 21:17).

For a priest, who wields the power Christ gave to his apostles, Peter stands as the center, unifying force, and director of his priestly ministry. *"Simon . . . you in your turn must strengthen your brothers"* (Luke 22:32). Such recognition of the Holy See has always been the special charism of the Society of Jesus, and the crown of the Jesuit vocation is its specific loyalty to the Pope.

The concerns of Peter in his unique apostolic service have comprised the substance of the vocation of Fr. John Hardon, S.J. Fr. Hardon is a man whose priesthood is shaped by a desire to respond to the needs of the Universal Church as they manifest themselves in the various circumstances of the Church in the United States. In all these circumstances he permits himself to the directed by the successor of Peter, thus insuring that his priestly vision and activity will be truly pertinent, truly universal, and truly Christian.

"The hardest thing in the world is to submit our will to the will of God," Fr. Hardon reflects. Nevertheless he has strived to make this submission the guiding principle of his life. But the will of God—or the will of anyone else for that matter—was a troublesome point for a fiercely independent boy who grew up in the shadows of the industrial mills and factories of Cleveland, Ohio.

John's father was an iron construction worker, and at the age of 26 he suffered a fatal accident, falling from a scaffold while on the job. The year was 1915, and young Anna Hardon found herself a widow with very little money and a one-year-old son.

She was, however, a woman of deep faith, a Franciscan tertiary who embraced her poverty and her difficult circumstances with courage and grace. Anna Hardon never remarried, but she raised and supported her only child by working as a cleaning woman, mopping, sweeping, and cleaning offices in the city. She would often work nights, spending her days keeping an eye on John. The boy was willful and self-possessed; he was determined that no one was going to tell him what to do.

Yet as he grew he also became deeply devoted to his mother, and her religious sense—which filled the home and dominated John's upbringing—made its mark upon him. Upon entering the house John or his mother would always say "Praised be Jesus Christ" to which the other would respond "Now and forever, Amen." There was a statue of the Virgin Mother of God, and always holy water by the front door. As is so often the case, the wealth of Christ that enriched their small home was accompanied by the poverty of the world. Mother and son could not afford a telephone; in fact they seldom bought a newspaper.

"... *correct them and guide them as the Lord does*" (Eph. 6:4). Anna Hardon was determined to raise her son as a dedicated and devoted Christian, imbued with a full appreciation for God's salvation and an abiding love for the Church. John was taught especially to love the priesthood, and to have a sense that priests extend the mission of Christ on earth. This vision of the priesthood, combined with his mother's unceasing example of life in the Spirit of God, drew John to reflect upon his own place in the pilgrimage of faith. His mother never openly suggested the priesthood to him; nevertheless from his earliest years it was a path that seemed particularly challenging. He desired to be of service to others, and the priesthood embodied the highest expression of service.

John Hardon was a boy with a strong desire for achievement, and with abilities that made all sorts of achievements possible. In school he excelled, consistently receiving the highest grades, and he developed a variety of interests. Priesthood, however, was always a factor, and as he grew he became aware of the different ways of dedicating oneself exclusively to the Gospel; ways that were a response to Christ who invites total commitment: *"If you would be perfect ..."* (Mt. 19:21).

As an eighth grader, John first heard of a way that seemed particularly inspiring to him. In his Church History class, he was struck by the story of St. Peter Canisius who preached the Gospel in the midst of a crisis of faith in 16th century Germany. St. Peter's life and work—so vibrant and so full of achievement—drew strength from his special commitment to a religious congregation called the Society of Jesus. *"Grow strong in the Lord, with the strength of his power"* (Eph. 6:10).

John was impressed with the Jesuit spirit, and he wanted to attend a Jesuit High School. His mother, however, barely made enough money to support the two of them, and the Jesuit school was simply too expensive. So he attended the diocesan high school of Cathedral Latin. Here John's thoughts of the priesthood became somewhat submerged in a host of other concerns. His mother's health began to fail, and he was convinced that he would have to build his future around the responsibility of caring for her. So he considered various professional careers, keeping in mind always his two driving—and perhaps at times conflicting—ambitions: to be of service to others and to "make his mark upon the world."

Teaching appealed to him; it certainly provided the opportunity to share knowledge and wisdom—even the depths of his faith—with others. Then there was the stage; John embarked upon an acting career while in high school that continued all the way through college. His interests in the sciences, however, as well as his interest in helping people attracted him to the medical profession.

Thus when John entered college any interest he had in the priesthood had to contend with his concern for his mother, his desire for a career and the various professions open to him, and finally—an interest that had been developing all along—his thoughts of eventual marriage and family. There was a girl he had known since his boyhood days who was intelligent, familiar, and devoted to the same ideals he himself possessed. She, it seemed, would make a very fine wife, should John decide that he wanted to get married. In facing all of these varying directions for his life John had one firm rule: no one else was going to make his decision for him.

"You know me through and through" (Ps. 139:14). In reflecting on these years, Fr. Hardon notes that a vocation "is a very special grace given by God to certain men." This grace, however, requires human cooperation or it will not come to fruition; in fact it may never even be discovered. In order for a man even to be aware that he is called to be "another Christ" he must respond to the purposeful movements of the Spirit.

Such "movements" became more compelling for John during his years at John Carroll University. He had at last obtained his wish to attend a school run by the Society of Jesus, and the Jesuit presence had a profound impact on him. There was a certain strength about the Jesuits, a "manliness" that John had never experienced at home because he never knew his father. Also their mental discipline impressed him; it motivated him to major in Philosophy and it began to shape his approach to spirituality through the direction of Fr. LeMay, a brilliant and discerning man who saw in John great potential.

Entering the Society, however, seemed out of the question. His mother's health was getting worse and John simply could not imagine leaving her to take care of herself. He had also applied and been accepted to Ohio State Medical School. And then there was the possibility of marriage. . . .

As a senior in college John had pretty much made up his mind that he was not suited for the priesthood. The two biggest influences in his life, however, caused him to reconsider. Fr. LeMay did not agree with John's assessment of his situation. After three years as his spiritual director, Fr. LeMay had reached a different conclusion: that John did indeed have a priestly vocation.

His mother had also discovered the depth of John's consideration of the priesthood. She had no intention of standing in the way of God's will for her son, and was confident that He would provide for her just as He does for all who seek His Kingdom. Knowing very well John's sensitivity about being pressured into doing anything, she never once urged him to become a priest. Instead she simply took him aside and informed him that he must not allow his mother to stand between him and the will of the Holy Spirit; indeed the very same God who was calling him would guard every hair on his mother's head. "Have a little more trust in my faith," she told him. *"If any man is thirsty, let him come to me"* (Jn 7:37).

John had reached the moment in his life when a decision had to be made. The strength of the Jesuits, their intellectual vigor, and their commitment to teaching seemed to embody all the things that John was looking for in a life of service, and a unique opportunity to share the faith; even the thought of marriage and family was overwhelmed by a realization of the spiritual family that springs up around a priest who brings the life of Christ to so many people.

Therefore John became determined to enter the Jesuit novitiate. There remained the very difficult matter of informing "the girl" of his decision; it appeared as though she was hoping they might get married, and in fact marriage had been discussed on several previous occasions. Less than a week before he was to enter the novitiate, John took her out to dinner at a nice restaurant in downtown Cleveland. There he revealed to her his plans and the mysterious and persistent call that had begun to mold his life. "I should have waited until the end of the meal," he recalls. She was understandably upset, but eventually she came to see the wisdom of his decision, and years later she remarked to him that he had "made the better choice."

On September 1, 1936, John Hardon entered the Society of Jesus, but less than two months into his novitiate he began to experience doubts. He felt once again that he had abandoned his mother when she most needed him. Troubled in spirit, John wrote to Fr. LeMay. The reply was swift and direct: "John, you belong in the Society of Jesus. What you are experiencing is a temptation. Put it out of your mind."

Thus advised, John set about banishing the temptation with stubborn determination. The intimate bond between him and his mother, he reasoned, obviously needed to be subordinate to the voice of the Spirit. Therefore after his novitiate—although they continued a frequent correspondence—John went seven years without visiting his mother. He finally broke this period of separation only because his superior ordered him to do so while he was a scholastic.

John's dedication to his seminary formation remained steady once his initial doubts were resolved. Within this formation he discovered a love for theology, and further developed his love for teaching. In 1941 he published his first article, on the study of Latin. That summer, during a lakeshore vacation, one of the scholastics drowned. His death touched John very deeply, and he told his superiors that he did not think that he could ever take another vacation. And he hasn't, to this very day.

Constant activity and corresponding achievement characterized John's years of theology at West Baden College in Indiana. He developed a profound desire to write and teach, but he also became very familiar with his strong self-will, and recognized the dangers it posed to the pursuit of his vocation. In light of this recognition, John was determined not to *request* further theological study; he would leave the determination of his future completely in the hands of the Holy Spirit. Thus his love for theology would not become an obstacle to his service to God.

On June 18, 1947 that service was sealed for eternity in the mark of the priesthood. *"Greater works than these shall you perform"* (Jn. 5:20). John Hardon was called to participate in the highest achievement in human history: the redemptive sacrifice of Jesus Christ. His participation, however, was such that the achievement was not a result of his own powers and determination of will. Rather his role lay precisely in his submission to the will of Jesus, in whom he would find his dignity and fruitfulness. In this way Fr. Hardon was required to embrace totally the very thing that he identifies as "hardest in the world"—following the will of God straight through to his very identity as "another Christ." It is to this Christ that he must attribute all accomplishment, yet in this Christ such accomplishment knows no limit. In the priesthood Fr. Hardon had found the union of his high ideals—and his high hopes—with the demands of holiness.

Anna Hardon saw her son ordained to the priesthood and rejoiced that God had brought so great a blessing into his life. A year later she died, but not before she heard that the Jesuit superiors had decided to send her son to Rome for advanced theological study.

The pursuit of Fr. Hardon's great love was destined to be a reality, and the fact that he had not initiated or suggested theological study convinced him all the more that the direction of his superiors was the will of God.

From 1949 to 1951 he studied graduate theology at the Gregorian University in Rome, receiving his S. T. D. and writing a dissertation based on his extensive research into the thought and writings of St. Robert Bellarmine. Fr. Hardon would have loved to remain in Rome to teach, but health problems forced him to return to the United States in 1951. Here he took a position on the faculty of West Baden College, and began to teach Jesuit theology students.

Fr. Hardon had hopes of doing missionary work, perhaps as a teacher at the newly opened Jesuit University in Tokyo. For health reasons, however, he was told by superiors to "forget about the missions." Nevertheless he was determined that, if he could not reach missionary lands in person, he would at least get there by the force of his teaching and writing. So he began to work a great deal in the field of comparative religion; in the study of oriental religions Fr. Hardon found not only areas that were compatible with Christianity but also sections of thought that were clearly influenced in a direct manner by contact with the Christian message.

Fr. Hardon brought the fruits of his extensive research into the classroom, teaching future Jesuit missionaries about the religious traditions and cultures that were waiting for them in the Far East. Thus he reached the missions in spirit, and fostered an increase in the understanding and evangelical zeal that anticipated the work and vision of the Second Vatican Council. *"Turn to me and be saved, all the ends of the earth, for I am God unrivaled"* (Is. 45:22).

During this same period Fr. Hardon began a study of the Protestant denominations that have built America's religious tradition. In 1956 he published a book, *Protestant Churches in America*, that gained such a high reputation for thoroughness and scholarship that it is used as a text in Protestant seminaries to this day.

Over the next several years Protestant seminaries and colleges began seeking Fr. Hardon as a visiting professor. Curiously enough, they wanted him to teach Catholic theology; they knew that he was familiar with American Protestantism and also that he was committed to an uncompromising Catholic perspective. While continuing his full-time post at West Baden, Fr. Hardon also accepted visiting professorships at a variety of Protestant schools, including Bethany School of Theology, Lutheran School of Theology, and Seabury-Western Divinity School. In this work he saw an opportunity to share the fullness of the faith with those baptized in Christ who, because of the circumstances of history, time and place, or culture, had yet to receive a complete understanding and appreciation of the Christian faith and of the Church that extends the power and presence of Jesus Christ. *"Who do you say I am"* (Lk. 9:20)?

Fr. Hardon's experiences in the Protestant seminary were very fruitful. Though his teaching alone did not often bring individuals into a full communion with the Catholic Church, he did find that his Protestant students gained a greater understanding of the Catholic faith, and even began to grasp the sense of the Catholic priesthood. He hoped that they would bring this understanding to bear upon their own Protestant ministries, thus leading their people to a deeper appreciation of the Gospel and a longing for a complete union with the Church; the union that Christ wills for all who are baptized in His name.

Moreover, Fr. Hardon's work in Protestant seminaries was in some respects monumental and ground-breaking. When he first accepted the position at Seabury-Western Divinity school, the Anglican Archbishop of Canterbury sent a personal representative to Chicago to commemorate the event: for the first time in history an Anglican/Episcopalian seminary had appointed a teacher who was a member of the once hated and feared Society of Jesus.

Fr. Hardon thus anticipated, and later fulfilled, the call to ecumenical dialogue expressed by the Second Vatican Council, and he did so in a manner that preserved continuity with the fullness of Catholic faith and embraced a fresh vitality; elements easily recognized before and after the Council by those attentive to the Spirit of Truth. *"For a man's words flow out of what fills his heart"* (Mt. 12:34).

For Fr. Hardon, the voice of the Holy Spirit had a particularly intimate connection to the words of the Vicar of Christ, not only as a loyal member of the Church but also as a Jesuit. In 1953 he pronounced his final vows, including the special vow of unwavering fidelity to the See of Peter. Henceforth the directives of the Pope took on a new and more deeply personal significance for Fr. Hardon in his vocation as a Jesuit priest. He must be one heart with the Holy Father, always seeking to work for the Universal Church within his own sphere, and in the particular churches he serves.

This work became particularly important in the years following Vatican II. From 1962 to 1967, Fr. Hardon taught Roman Catholicism and Comparative Religion at Western Michigan University, where he completed and published his book, *Religions of the World*, in 1963. In 1967 he returned to teaching Jesuit scholastics at two Jesuit theological schools in Illinois and he later added a visiting professorship at St. Paul University in Ottawa, Canada, teaching missiology to missionaries on furlough. During this whole time the Church in America was undergoing a period of immense trial. Two areas of the Church were particularly affected: consecrated life and academic life. Both were afflicted by numerous temptations against the unity of the Church, a sense of Christian purpose, and faith itself.

"The Spirit too comes to help us in our weakness" (Rom. 8:26). In the midst of this disturbance of mind and heart, Fr. Hardon—steeped as he is in both the consecrated life and the academic life—discerned the key to weathering the storm. It is the same unifying component that directed his own vocation and that, ultimately, is the central element in the call of every Christian to conform his will to the will of the Father in Christ Jesus; the key is loyalty to the Bishop of Rome.

In 1967 Fr. Hardon began regular consultation with the

Congregations for Religious and the Clergy in Rome. Sensitive to the needs of the Church in America, Fr. Hardon cooperated with Congregations in searching for ways to implement an authentic ecclesial renewal in the United States. Fr. Hardon accepted the task of assisting in the organization of several important projects that touched upon religious life, academics, and catechesis.

In 1969 he helped organize the *Consortium Perfectae Caritatis*, a union of religious who are dedicated to their consecrated vocation and its witness of Christian perfection, and who are devoted to the Holy Father and the unity of the Church. In 1973 he helped organize the Institute on Religious Life, which today includes 30,000 members from 135 religious communities.

In 1971 Fr. Hardon and a group of clergy and laity met with Ugo Modotti, a Camaldolese Abbot who had been sent to America by Pope Paul VI with a special commission to establish a Catholic Media Organization. Fr. Modotti grew to trust Fr. Hardon and, one night over dinner, requested that Fr. Hardon take over his commission in the event that anything should happen to him. Two weeks later Fr. Modotti died. Armed with a commission from the Holy Father Fr. Hardon plunged into the media apostolate, assisting in the founding of Mark Communications in Canada in 1972. He also began gathering support for media work in the United States.

Meanwhile there remained much work to be done in the field of education. The Holy See wished to establish a series of Pontifical Catechetical Institutes in the United States in order to insure that religious educators receive a clear understanding of the Christian faith they are called to communicate. Fr. Hardon leant support and assistance to those who worked to establish these institutions, most notably Msgr. Eugene Kevane. And in 1974 Fr. Hardon became a full-time professor at the Institute for Advanced Studies in Catholic Doctrine at St. John's University in New York City.

In connection with the need for comprehensive and faithful catechesis, Fr. Hardon committed himself to two significant publications. He cooperated with the Sisters of Notre Dame of Chardon, Ohio to produce a religious textbook series for elementary school called *Christ Our Life*. Loyola University Press published the first edition in 1976 and a revised edition in 1985. Today the *Christ Our Life* series is used by over six hundred thousand students throughout the United States.

For adults, teachers, and fellow priests, Fr. Hardon wrote an extensive volume called simply *The Catholic Catechism*. Published in 1975, this work was written to reflect the authentic implementation of Vatican II and to assist all who desire to present the faith according to the mind of the Church. *"This is doctrine you can rely on"* (Titus 3:8).

Today Fr. Hardon is well established as a theology professor at St. John's University, and he continues his dedication to catechetical work. In 1982 he participated in the establishment of the Catholic Home Study Institute, which provides training in catechetics all across the country by correspondence and with the aid of audio-visual techniques. And in 1980 he succeeded in forming an organization dedicated to the Media Apostolate. The Catholic Voice of America, affiliated with the Notre Dame Pontifical Institute in Arlington, Virginia, began operation in October of 1986. One of the prime purposes of C. V. A. is to facilitate extensive training for teachers of religion by means of the media. Fr. Hardon hopes that this organization will fulfill the commission he received from the Pope, through the hands of Fr. Modotti.

"Keep on working at the Lord's work always, knowing that, in the Lord, you cannot be laboring in vain" (1 Cor. 15:58). Fr. Hardon recently celebrated the fiftieth anniversary of his entry into the Society of Jesus. In reflecting on these years, he focuses on the priesthood that has been given to him. Fr. Hardon notes that the priesthood is not just a job; rather it is "the possession of extraordinary power, especially the power to make the Eucharist and therefore Christ's real presence on earth possible,

and the power of remitting sins." It is because of the priesthood that Christ is present on earth both physically in the Eucharist and mystically in the Church. Therefore it is important that, when they are ordained, priests realize *who they are*. This realization should grow as the priest progresses in his vocation, and should inform all his activities. As a teacher for 35 years, Fr. Hardon has developed a keen awareness of the fact that he is a priest even in the classroom. Because of the power of orders, the priest possesses a special charism—like Christ Himself—to enlighten minds and strengthen wills in the supernatural dimension. Thus he can bring his priesthood to bear upon his teaching and his apostolic work.

Fr. Hardon sees the spirit of the priesthood as an all-encompassing sense of mission. "The priest must want to share," he says, "to wear himself out in sharing." This spirit is truly universal, reaching out to embrace all of God's people, with a profound consciousness of their needs and an appreciation of their destiny in Christ. With the Vicar of Christ as his constant inspiration and source of direction, Fr. Hardon continues to dedicate his life, in a spirit of self-sacrifice, to the service of the Church, making the power of Christ present and the truth of Christ clear for all those who seek eternal life.

Conclusion

"*Jesus said to them, 'Come after me; I will make you fishers of men'* " (Mk. 1:17). These words, spoken by God deep within the heart of every priest at the dawn of his vocation, reveal the essence of the calling to priesthood. For here Jesus reveals the priesthood as not simply a job or a collection of activities, but rather as an *identity*, the substance of which is conformity to Himself and service to the humanity destined by God for adopted sonship.

What does it mean to "come after me," to become like Jesus Christ? These pages have attempted to illustrate the likeness to Christ that underlies every priestly vocation; that molds and shapes it, applying a Christlike quality to every priestly act. Jesus Christ is the Redeemer of man; it is He alone who makes it possible for human beings to achieve the fulfillment for which they are made, to satisfy the desire that God has placed in each of their hearts. This fulfillment is the life of Christ Himself, who raises His members to eternal life in the Holy Spirit, to the glory of God the Father.

The priest's identity, then, is conformed to that of Christ the Redeemer. We have seen how the ministry of every priest is fundamentally oriented toward other people; to talk about the life of a priest is to talk about the people whose lives have been affected by his work. His service to the Christian people, moreover, is not just a temporary provision for their well being; it is

above all else a permanent and central force in the very purpose of their existence. As the redeeming Christ, the priest is
the most important person in his community; this is not because
of any greatness of his own, but rather because he makes possible the Christian life—the Christian vocation—for all the people in his care.

   *"This is my commandment: Love one another, as I have loved
you"* (John 15:12). This universal Christian vocation is at its deepest level a *call to love*. And because Christian love is first a love
of God, it stands also as a love of man in the full context of his
destiny to live eternally with God, a destiny made real by the
love of Christ. The priest makes Christian love possible because
he makes Christ *present* in every place he serves.

   "Yes, God so loved the world, that he gave his only Son . . ."
(John 3:16). Each priest, then, has a pivotal task within the
Church and a mission to the world: He must witness to the fundamental truth that Jesus Christ is God in the flesh. His testimony requires above all a profound interior union with the
Church, the Body of Christ on earth today. This union is ef-
fected in the Eucharist—the central element of his ministry—and solidified by the teaching authority and authentic
leadership to which the priest must always remain faithful,
meeting Christ in the poverty of obedience. This "poverty" is
above all a constant willingness to conform himself to the will
of the Father in Christ Jesus, a readiness to become all things to
all men in an effort to serve Jesus in His desire to touch the
multitude. As the fidelity of the priests we have met in this
book illustrates, this poverty of spirit is the force behind a joyful and prompt obedience to the voice of Christ, the direction
of the Spirit.

   God's call to love, fulfilled in the obedience of Christ, requires the priest to embrace his duties in the spirit of sacrificial
love. This spirit, besides being his own response to the universal
call to live the Christian life, stands as the underlying force behind his particular pastoral mission. The priest is presented with

the challenge of instilling holiness in his people through his own personal witness and sacrifice, as well as his sacramental and preaching ministry, so that they may in turn extend the power of Christ according to their own mission to renew the everyday world. The priest is the leader through whom Christ directs the whole mission of the Church in particular places and circumstances.

The variety of these circumstances, and their often ordinary nature, is perhaps the most revealing characteristic in the life of a priest. His success is not measured by the visible stature of his deeds but rather by the depth of his love, and the degree to which he recognizes and manifests the presence of Jesus Christ. To this end the priest must see in the circumstances of his ministry the hidden Jesus. In his faithfulness to the reality that the Son of God has indeed been made man, the priest continually finds himself face to face with the Mother of God; the Blessed Virgin Mary comes to him each day bringing the Christ child in her womb, a child waiting to be born anew in countless hearts; and a child that represents the hidden power of his ministry. Like Elizabeth, he responds to this presence with humility and praise: *"Blessed is the fruit of your womb"* (Lk. 1:42). It is this hidden Christ that he must so often follow, placing himself also—like the child to whom he is called to conform himself in every priestly action—under the protection and motherly care of the Virgin, realizing that He who is mighty has indeed done great things for her.

Thus the priest moves forward in the journey of the People of God, a pilgrimage to the Father which he must make himself, as a disciple of Christ, but which he must also lead, as a sharer in the high priesthood of Christ. The personal history of each priest is bound up with his search for ways to actualize the Christian vocations of people; in this sense he truly "fishes for men," drawing them ever more fully into the net of the Kingdom of God, ever closer to their full identity in Christ.

"Love bears all things, believes all things, hopes all things, endures all things. Love does not come to an end" (1 Cor. 13:7-8). This Christian identity, in its most profound dimension, represents a share in universal and infinite Love—Love from God and for God, drawing together all of the faithful and reaching out to the entire human race. The priests in these profiles, and all priests like them, are important because their ministry touches upon the beginning and the increase of the love that vivifies God's people. In this love Christ is continually doing the will of His Father, which is quite simply to *save the world*; it is a love that knows no boundaries and no limits to its intensity, a love that pours out from the Church and seeks every member of a crippled and suffering humanity, a love that cries out from the very heart of the redemption, *"Father, into your hands I commend my spirit."*

What power has been placed in the hands of a priest! And what a commission has been given to him—he holds the Church of Christ together in love, a Church that is the manifestation of God's power and the sign of the union He wills for the whole of humanity. The priest thus bears with him the promise of the Holy Spirit—that every human being is called to live forever in the love of God, a life that renews the depths of man in spirit and in truth, and a love that burns secretly in the work of every devoted priest just as it did in the heart of Jesus Christ on the cross, a hidden flame that will one day burst forth and enkindle the world. *"And when I am lifted up from the earth, I shall draw all men to myself"* (John 12:32).

Appendix

Pope John Paul II greets Fr. Robert J. Fox, head of Trinity's
Vocations Support Program.

Letter of Pope John Paul II
To All the Priests of the Church
For Holy Thursday 1986

Dear Brother Priests,

Holy Thursday, the Feast of Priests

1.   Here we are again, about to celebrate Holy Thursday, the day on which Christ Jesus instituted the Eucharist and at the same time our ministerial Priesthood. "Having loved his own who were in the world, he loved them to the end."[1] As the Good Shepherd, he was about to give his life for his sheep,[2] to save man, to reconcile him with his Father and bring him into a new life. And already at the Last Supper he offered to the Apostles as food his own Body given up for them, and his Blood shed for them.

Each year this day is an important one for all Christians: like the first disciples they come to receive the Body and Blood of Christ in the evening liturgy that renews the Last Supper.

---

[1]Jn 13:1.
[2]Cf. Jn 10:11.

They receive from the Savior his testament of fraternal love which must inspire their whole lives, and they begin to watch with him, in order to be united with him in his Passion. You yourselves gather them together and guide their prayer.

But this day is especially important for us, dear brother priests. It is the feast of priests. It is the birthday of our Priesthood, which is a sharing in the one Priesthood of Christ the Mediator. On this day the priests of the whole world are invited to concelebrate the Eucharist with their bishops and with them to renew the promises of their priestly commitment to the service of Christ and his Church.

As you know, I feel particularly close to each one of you on this occasion. And, the same as every year, as a sign of our sacramental union in the same Priesthood, and impelled by my affectionate esteem for you and by my duty to confirm all my brothers in their service of the Lord, I wish to send you this letter to help you to stir up the wonderful gift that was conferred on you through the laying on of hands.[3] This ministerial Priesthood which is our lot is also our vocation and our grace. It marks our whole life with the seal of the most necessary and most demanding of services, the salvation of souls. We are led to it by a host of predecessors.

The matchless example of the Curé of Ars

2.   One of those predecessors remains particularly present in the memory of the Church, and he will be especially commemorated this year, on the second centenary of his birth: *Saint John Mary Vianney, the Curé of Ars.*

Together we wish to thank Christ, the Prince of Pastors, for this extraordinary model of priestly life and service which the saintly Curé of Ars offers to the whole Church, and above all to us priests.

---

[3]Cf. 2 Tim 1:6.

How many of us prepared ourselves for the Priesthood, or today exercise the difficult task of caring for souls, having before our eyes the figure of Saint John Mary Vianney! His example cannot be forgotten. More than ever we need his witness, his intercession, in order to face the situations of our times when, in spite of a certain number of hopeful signs, evangelization is being contradicted by a growing secularization, when spiritual discipline is being neglected, when many are losing sight of the Kingdom of God, when often, even in the pastoral ministry, there is a too exclusive concern for the social aspect, for temporal aims. In the last century the Curé of Ars had to face difficulties which were perhaps of a different kind but which were no less serious. By his life and work he represented, for the society of his time, a great evangelical challenge that bore astonishing fruits of conversion. Let us not doubt that he still represents to us today that *great evangelical challenge.*

I therefore invite you now to meditate on our Priesthood in the presence of this matchless pastor who illustrates both the fullest realization of the priestly ministry and the holiness of the minister.

As you know, John Mary Baptist Vianney died at Ars on 4 August 1859, after some forty years of exhausting dedication. He was seventy-three years of age. When he arrived, Ars was a small and obscure village in the Diocese of Lyons, now in the Diocese of Belley. At the end of his life, people came from all over France, and his reputation for holiness, after he had been called home to God, soon attracted the attention of the universal Church. Saint Pius X beatified him in 1905, Pius XI canonized him in 1925, and then in 1929 declared him Patron Saint of the parish priests of the whole world. On the centenary of his death, Pope John XXIII wrote the Encyclical *Nostri Sacerdotii Primitias,* to present the Curé of Ars as a model of priestly life and asceticism, a model of piety and Eucharistic worship, a model of pastoral zeal, and this in the context of the needs of our time. Here, I would simply like to draw your attention to

certain essential points so as to help us to rediscover and live
our Priesthood better.

The Truly Extraordinary Life
of the Curate of Ars

His tenacious will in preparing for the Priesthood

3.   The Curé of Ars is truly a model of strong will for those
preparing for the Priesthood. Many of the trials which followed
one after another could have discouraged him: the effects of the
upheaval of the French Revolution, the lack of opportunities
for education in his rural environment, the reluctance of his father, the need for him to do his share of work in the fields, the
hazards of military service. Above all, and in spite of his intuitive intelligence and lively sensitivity, there was his great difficulty in learning and memorizing, and so in following the theological courses in Latin, all of which resulted in his dismissal
from the seminary in Lyons. However, after the genuineness of
his vocation had finally been acknowledged, at 29 years of age
he was able to be ordained. Through his tenacity in working and
praying, he overcame all obstacles and limitations, just as he did
later in his priestly life, by his perseverance in laboriously
preparing his sermons or spending the evenings reading the
works of theologians and spiritual writers. From his youth he
was filled with a great desire to "win souls for the good God" by
being a priest, and he was supported by the confidence placed
in him by the parish priest of the neighboring town of Ecully,
who never doubted his vocation and took charge of a good part
of his training. What an example of courage for those who today experience the grace of being called to the Priesthood!

The depth of his love for Christ and for souls

4. The Curé of Ars is a model of priestly zeal for all pastors. The secret of his generosity is to be found without doubt in *his love of God,* lived without limits, in constant response to the love made manifest *in Christ crucified.* This is where he bases his desire to do everything to save the souls ransomed by Christ at such a great price, and to bring them back to the love of God. Let us recall one of those pithy sayings which he had the knack of uttering: "The priesthood is the love of the Heart of Jesus."[4] In his sermons and catechesis he continually returned to that love: "O my God, I prefer to die loving you than to live a single instant without loving you. . . . I love you, my Divine Savior, because you were crucified for us . . . because you have me crucified for you."[5]

For the sake of Christ, he seeks to conform himself exactly to the radical demands that Jesus in the Gospel puts before the disciples whom he sends out: prayer, poverty, humility, self-denial, voluntary penance. And, like Christ, he has a love for his flock that leads him to extreme pastoral commitment and self-sacrifice. Rarely has a pastor been so acutely aware of his responsibilities, so consumed by a desire to wrest his people from their sins or their lukewarmness. "O my God, grant me the conversion of my parish: I consent to suffer whatever you wish, for as long as I live."

Dear brother priests, nourished by the Second Vatican Council which has felicitously placed the priest's consecration within the framework of his pastoral mission, let us join Saint John Mary Vianney and seek the dynamism of our pastoral zeal

---

[4]Cf. *Jean-Marie Vianney, curé d'ars, sa pensée, son coeur,* présentés par l'Abbé Bernard Nodet, éditions Xavier Mappus, Le Puy, 1958, p. 100; henceforth quoted as: Nodet.
[5]Nodet, p. 44.

in the Heart of Jesus, in his love for souls. If we do not draw from the same source, our ministry risks bearing little fruit!

The many wonderful fruits of his ministry

5.   In the case of the Curé of Ars, the results were indeed wonderful, somewhat as with Jesus in the Gospel. Through John Mary Vianney, who consecrates his whole strength and his whole heart to him, Jesus saves souls. The Savior entrusts them to him, in abundance.

First *his parish*—which numbered only 230 people when he arrived—which will be profoundly changed. One recalls that in that village there was a great deal of indifference and very little religious practice among the men. The bishop had warned John Mary Vianney: "There is not much love of God in that parish; you will put some there." But quite soon, far beyond his own village the Curé becomes *the pastor of a multitude* coming from the entire region, from different parts of France and from other countries. It is said that 80,000 came in the year 1858! People sometimes waited for days to see him, to go to confession to him. What attracted them to him was not merely curiosity nor even a reputation justified by miracles and extraordinary cures, which the saint would wish to hide. It was much more the realization of meeting a saint, amazing for his penance, so close to God in prayer, remarkable for his peace and humility in the midst of popular acclaim, and above all so intuitive in responding to the inner disposition of souls and in freeing them from their burdens, especially in the confessional. Yes, God chose as a model for pastors one who could have appeared poor, weak, defenseless and contemptible in the eyes of men.[6] He graced him with his best gifts as a guide and healer of souls.

---

[6]Cf. 1 Cor 1:28-29.

While recognizing the special nature of the grace given to the Curé of Ars, is there not here a sign of hope for pastors today who are suffering from a kind of spiritual desert?

The Main Acts of the Ministry
of the Curate of Ars

Different apostolic approaches to what is essential

6. John Mary Vianney dedicated himself essentially to teaching the faith and to purifying consciences, and these two ministries were directed towards the Eucharist. Should we not see here, today also, the three objectives of the priest's pastoral service?

While the purpose is undoubtedly to bring the people of God together around the Eucharistic mystery by means of catechesis and penance, other apostolic approaches, varying according to circumstances, are also necessary. Sometimes it is a simple presence, over the years, with the silent witness of faith in the midst of non-Christian surroundings; or being near to people, to families and their concerns; there is a preliminary evangelization that seeks to awaken to the faith unbelievers and the lukewarm; there is the witness of charity and justice shared with Christian lay people, which makes the faith more credible and puts it into practice. These give rise to a whole series of undertakings and apostolic works which prepare or continue Christian formation. The Curé of Ars himself taxed his ingenuity to devise initiatives adapted to his time and his parishioners. However, all these priestly activities were centered on the Eucharist, catechesis and the Sacrament of Reconciliation.

The Sacrament of Reconciliation

7.   It is undoubtedly his untiring devotion to the Sacrament of Reconciliation which revealed the principle charism of the Curé

of Ars and is rightly the reason for his renown. It is good that such an example should encourage us today to restore to the ministry of reconciliation all the attention which it deserves and which the Synod of Bishops of 1983 so justly emphasized.[7] Without the step of conversion, penance and seeking pardon that the Church's ministers ought untiringly to encourage and welcome, the much desired renewal will remain superficial and illusory.

The first care of the Curé of Ars was to teach the faithful to desire repentance. He stressed the beauty of God's forgiveness. Was not all his priestly life and all his strength dedicated to the conversion of sinners? And it was above all in the confessional that God's mercy manifested itself. So he did not wish to get rid of the penitents who came from all parts and to whom he often devoted ten hours a day, sometimes fifteen or more. For him this was undoubtedly the greatest of his mortifications, a form of martyrdom. In the first place it was a martyrdom in the physical sense from the heat, the cold or the suffocating atmosphere. Secondly in the moral sense, for he himself suffered from the sins confessed and even more the lack of repentance: "I weep because you do not weep." In the face of these indifferent people, whom he welcomed as best he could and tried to awaken in them the love of God, the Lord enabled him to reconcile great sinners who were repentant, and also to guide to perfection souls thirsting for it. It was here above all that God asked him to share in the Redemption.

For our own part, we have rediscovered, better than during the last century, the community aspect of penance, preparation for forgiveness and thanksgiving after forgiveness. But sacramental forgiveness will always require a personal encounter with the crucified Christ through the mediation of his

---

[7]Cf. John Paul II, Post-Synodal Apostolic Exhortation *Reconciliatio et paenitentia* (2 December 1984): *AAS* 77 (1985), pp. 185-275.

minister.[8] Unfortunately it is often the case that penitents do not fervently hasten to the confessional, as in the time of the Curé of Ars. Now, just when a great number seem to stay away from confession completely, for various reasons, it is a sign of the urgent need to develop a whole pastoral strategy of the Sacrament of Reconciliation. This will be done by constantly reminding Christians of the need to have a real relationship with God, to have a sense of sin when one is closed to God and to others, the need to be converted and through the Church to receive forgiveness as a free gift of God. They also need to be reminded of the conditions that enable the sacrament to be celebrated well, and in this regard to overcome prejudices, baseless fears and routine.[9] Such a situation at the same time requires that we ourselves should remain very available for this ministry of forgiveness, ready to devote to it the necessary time and care, and I would even say giving it priority over other activities. The faithful will then realize the value that we attach to it, as did the Curé of Ars.

Of course, as I wrote in the Post-Synodal Exhortation on Penance,[10] the ministry of reconciliation undoubtedly remains the most difficult, the most delicate, the most taxing and the most demanding of all—especially when priests are in short supply. This ministry also presupposes on the part of the confessor great human qualities, above all an intense and sincere spiritual life; it is necessary that the priest himself should make regular use of this sacrament.

Always be convinced of this, dear brother priests: this ministry of mercy is one of the most beautiful and most consoling. It enables you to enlighten consciences, to forgive them

---

[8]Cf. John Paul II, encyclical Letter *Redemptor hominis* (4 March 1979), No. 20: *AAS* 71 (1979), pp. 313-316.

[9]Cf. John Paul II, Post-Synodal Apostolic Exhortation *Reconciliatio et paenitentia* (2 December 1984), No. 28: *AAS* 77 (1985), pp. 250-252.

[10]Cf. *Ibid.*, No. 29: *AAS* 77 (1985), pp. 252-256.

and to give them fresh vigour in the name of the Lord Jesus. It enables you to be for them a spiritual physician and counsellor; it remains "the irreplaceable manifestation and the test of the priestly ministry."[11]

The Eucharist: offering the Mass, communion, adoration

8.   The two Sacraments of Reconciliation and the Eucharist remain closely linked. Without a continually renewed conversion and the reception of the sacramental grace of forgiveness, participation in the Eucharist would not reach its full redemptive efficacy.[12] Just as Christ began his ministry with the words "Repent and believe in the gospel,"[13] so the Curé of Ars generally began each of his days with the ministry of forgiveness. But he was happy to direct his reconciled penitents to the *Eucharist.*

The Eucharist was at the very center of his spiritual life and pastoral work. He said: "All good works put together are not equivalent to the Sacrifice of the Mass, because they are the works of men and the Holy Mass is the work of God."[14] It is in the Mass that the sacrifice of Calvary is made present for the Redemption of the world. Clearly, the priest must unite the daily gift of himself to the offering of the Mass: "How well a priest does, therefore, to offer himself to God in sacrifice every morning!"[15] "Holy Communion and the Holy Sacrifice of the Mass are the two most efficacious actions for obtaining the conversion of hearts."[16]

---

[11]John Paul II, Letter to Priests for Holy Thursday 1983, No. 3: *AAS* 75 (1983), pars I, p. 419.
[12]Cf. John Paul II, Encyclical Letter *Redemptor hominis* (4 March 1979), No. 20: *AAS* 71 (1979), p. 309-313.
[13]Mk 1:15.
[14]Nodet, p. 108.
[15]Nodet, p. 107.
[16]Nodet, p. 110.

Thus the Mass was for John Mary Vianney the great joy and comfort of his priestly life. He took great care, despite the crowds of penitents, to spend more than a quarter of an hour in silent preparation. He celebrated with recollection, clearly expressing his adoration at the consecration and communion. He accurately remarked: "The cause of priestly laxity is not paying attention to the Mass!"[17]

The Curé of Ars was particularly mindful of the permanence of Christ's real presence in the Eucharist. It was generally before the tabernacle that he spent long hours in adoration, before daybreak or in the evening; it was towards the tabernacle that he often turned during his homilies, saying with emotion: "He is there!" It was also for this reason that he, so poor in his presbytery, did not hesitate to spend large sums on embellishing his Church. The appreciable result was that his parishioners quickly took up the habit of coming to pray before the Blessed Sacrament, discovering, through the attitude of their pastor, the grandeur of the mystery of faith.

With such a testimony before our eyes, we think about what the Second Vatican Council says to us today on the subject of priests: "They exercise this sacred function of Christ most of all in the Eucharistic liturgy."[18] And more recently, the Extraordinary Synod in December 1985 recalled: "The liturgy must favor and make shine brightly the sense of the sacred. It must be imbued with reverence, adoration and glorification of God ... The Eucharist is the source and summit of all the Christian life."[19]

Dear brother priests, the example of the Curé of Ars invites us to a serious examination of conscience: what place do we give to the Mass in our daily lives? Is it, as on the day of our

---

[17]Nodet, p. 108.

[18]Second Vatican Council, Dogmatic Constitution on the Church *Lumen gentium,* No. 28.

[19]II, B, b/1 and C/1; cf. Second Vatican Council, Dogmatic Constitution on the Church *Lumen gentium,* No. 11.

192 JOHN M. JANARO

Ordination—it was our first act as priests!—the principle of our apostolic work and personal sanctification? What care do we take in preparing for it? And in celebrating it? In praying before the Blessed Sacrament? In encouraging our faithful people to do the same? In making our Churches the House of God to which the divine presence attracts the people of our time who too often have the impression of a world empty of God?

Preaching and Catechesis

9.   The Curé of Ars was also careful never to neglect in any way the ministry of the Word, which is absolutely necessary in predisposing people to faith and conversion. He even said: "Our Lord, who is truth itself, considers his Word no less important than his Body."[20] We know how long he spent, especially at the beginning, in laboriously composing his Sunday sermons. Later on he came to express himself more spontaneously, always with lively and clear conviction, with images and comparisons taken from daily life and easily grasped by his flock. His catechetical instructions to the children also formed an important part of his ministry, and the adults gladly joined the children so as to profit from this matchless testimony which flowed from his heart.

He had the courage to denounce evil in all its forms; he did not keep silent, for it was a question of the eternal salvation of his faithful people: "If a pastor remains silent when he sees God insulted and souls going astray, woe to him! If he does not want to be damned, and if there is some disorder in his parish, he must trample upon human respect and the fear of being despised or hated." This responsibility was his anguish as parish priest. But as a rule, "he preferred to show the attractive side of virtue rather than the ugliness of vice," and if he spoke—sometimes in tears—about sin and the danger for salvation, he insisted on the tenderness of God who has been of-

---

[20]Nodet, p. 126.

fended, and the happiness of being loved by God, united to God, living in His presence and for Him.

Dear brother priests, you are deeply convinced of the importance of proclaiming the Gospel, which the Second Vatican Council placed in the first rank of the functions of a priest.[21] You seek, through catechesis, through preaching and in other forms which also include the media, to touch the hearts of our contemporaries, with their hopes and uncertainties, in order to awaken and foster faith. Like the Curé of Ars and in accordance with the exhortation of the Council,[22] take care to teach the Word of God itself which calls people to conversion and holiness.

The Identity of the Priest

The specific ministry of the priest

10.   Saint John Mary Vianney gives an eloquent answer to certain *questionings of the priest's identity,* which have manifested themselves in the course of the last twenty years; in fact it seems that today a more balanced position is being reached.

The priest always, and in an unchangeable way, finds the source of his identity in Christ the Priest. It is not the world which determines his status, as though it depended on changing needs or ideas about social roles. The priest is marked with the seal of the Priesthood of Christ, in order to share in his function as the one Mediator and Redeemer.

So, because of this fundamental bond, there opens before the priest the immense field of the service of souls, for their salvation in Christ and in the Church. This service must be completely inspired by love of souls in imitation of Christ who gives his life for them. It is God's wish that all people should be

---

[21]Second Vatican Council, Decree on the Ministry and Life of Priests *Presbyterorum ordinis,* No. 4.
[22]Cf. *Ibid.*

saved, and that none of the little ones should be lost.[23] "The priest must always be ready to respond to the needs of souls," said the Curé of Ars.[24] "He is not for himself, he is for you."[25]

The priest is for the laity: he animates them and supports them in the exercise of the common priesthood of the baptized—so well illustrated by the Second Vatican Council—which consists in their making their lives a spiritual offering, in witnessing to the Christian spirit in the family, in taking charge of the temporal sphere and sharing in the evangelization of their brethren. But the service of the priest belongs to another order. He is ordained to act in the name of Christ the Head, to bring people into the new life made accessible by Christ, to dispense to them the mysteries—the Word, forgiveness, the Bread of Life—to gather them into his Body, to help them to form themselves from within, to live and to act according to the saving plan of God. In a word, our identity as priests is manifested in the "creative" exercise of the love for souls communicated by Christ Jesus.

Attempts to make the priest more like the laity are damaging to the Church. This does not mean in any way that the priest can remain remote from the human concerns of the laity: he must be very near to them, as John Mary Vianney was, but as a priest, always in a perspective which is that of their salvation and of the progress of the Kingdom of God. He is the witness and dispenser of a life other than earthly life.[26] It is essential to the Church that the identity of the priest be safeguarded, with its vertical dimension. The life and personality of the Curé of Ars are a particularly enlightening and vigorous illustration of this.

---

[23]Cf. Mt 18:14.
[24]Nodet, p. 101.
[25]Nodet, p. 102.
[26]Cf. Second Vatican Council, Decree on the Ministry and Life of Priests *Presbyterorum ordinis,* No. 3.

*His intimate configuration to Christ
and his solidarity with sinners*

11. Saint John Mary Vianney did not content himself with the ritual carrying out of the activities of his ministry. It was his heart and his life which he sought to conform to Christ.

Prayer was the soul of his life: silent and contemplative prayer, generally in his church at the foot of the tabernacle. Through Christ, his soul opened to the three divine Persons, to whom he would entrust "his poor soul" in his last will and testament. "He kept a constant union with God in the middle of an extremely busy life." And he did not neglect the office or the rosary. He turned spontaneously to the Virgin.

His *poverty* was extraordinary. He literally stripped himself of everything for the poor. And he shunned honors. *Chastity* shone in his face. He knew the value of purity in order "to rediscover the source of love which is God." *Obedience* to Christ consisted, for John Mary Vianney, in obedience to the Church and especially to the Bishop. This obedience took the form of accepting the heavy charge of being a parish priest, which often frightened him.

But the Gospel insists especially on *renouncing self,* on accepting the Cross. Many were the crosses which presented themselves to the Curé of Ars in the course of his ministry: calumny on the part of the people, being misunderstood by an assistant priest or other confréres, contradictions, and also a mysterious struggle against the powers of hell, and sometimes even the temptation to despair in the midst of spiritual darkness.

Nonetheless he did not content himself with just accepting these trials without complaining; he went beyond them by *mortification,* imposing on himself continual fasts and many other rugged practices in order "to reduce his body to servitude," as Saint Paul says. But what we must see clearly in this penance, which our age unhappily has little taste for, are his motives: love of God and the conversion of sinners. Thus he asks a discouraged fellow priest: "You have prayed . . . , you have wept . . . , but have you fasted, have you kept vigil. . . ?"[27] Here we are close to the warning of Jesus to the Apostles: "But this kind is cast out only by prayers and fasting."[28]

In a word, John Mary Vianney sanctified himself so as to be more able to sanctify others. Of course, conversion remains the secret of hearts, which are free in their actions, and the secret of God's grace. By his ministry, the priest can only enlighten people, guide them in the internal forum and give them the sacraments. The sacraments are of course actions of Christ, and their effectiveness is not diminished by the imperfection or unworthiness of the minister. But the results depend also on the dispositions of those who receive them, and these are greatly assisted by the personal holiness of the priest, by his perceptible witness, as also by the mysterious exchange of merits in the Communion of Saints. Saint Paul said: "In my flesh I complete what is lacking in Christ's afflictions for the sake of his body, that is, the Church."[29] John Mary Vianney in a sense wished to force God to grant these graces of conversion, not only by his prayer but by the sacrifice of his whole life. He wished to love God for those who did not love him, and even do the penance which they would not do. He was truly a pastor completely at one with his sinful people.

Dear brother priests, let us not be afraid of this very personal commitment—marked by asceticism and inspired by love—which God asks of us for the proper exercise of our Priesthood. Let us remember the recent reflections of the Synodal Fathers: "It seems to us that in the difficulties of today God wishes to teach us more deeply the value, importance and cen-

---

[27]Nodet, p. 193.
[28]Mt 17:21.
[29]Col 1:24.

tral place of the Cross of Jesus Christ."[30] In the priest, Christ re-
lives his passion, for the sake of souls. Let us give thanks to God
who thus permits us to share in the Redemption, in our hearts
and in our flesh!

For all these reasons, Saint John Mary Vianney never
ceases to be a witness, ever living, ever relevant, to the truth
about the priestly vocation and service. We recall the convincing way in which he spoke of the greatness of the priest and of
the absolute need for him. Those who are already priests, those
who are preparing for the Priesthood and those who will be
called to it must fix their eyes on his example and follow it. The
faithful too will more clearly grasp, thanks to him, the mystery
of the Priesthood of their priests. No, *the figure of the Curé of
Ars does not fade.*

Conclusion: for Holy Thursday

12.   Dear Brothers, may these reflections renew your joy at
being priests, your desire to be priests more profoundly! the
witness of the Curé of Ars contains still other treasures to be
discovered. We shall return to these themes at greater length
during the pilgrimage which I shall have the joy of making next
October, since the French Bishops have invited me to Ars in
honor of the second centenary of the birth of John Mary
Vianney.

I address this first meditation to you, dear brothers, for
the Solemnity of Holy Thursday. In each of our diocesan
communities we are going to gather together, on this birthday
of our Priesthood, to renew the grace of the Sacrament of
Orders, to stir up the love which is the mark of our vocation.

We hear Christ saying to us as he said to the Apostles:
"Greater love has no man than this, that a man lay down his life

---

[30]Final Report, ID/2.

for his friend. . . . No longer do I call you servants . . . , I have called you friends."[31]

Before him who manifests love in its fullness, we, priests and Bishops, renew our priestly commitments.

We pray for one another, each for his brother, and all for all.

We ask the eternal Father that the memory of the Curé of Ars may help to stir up our zeal in his service.

We beseech the Holy Spirit to call to the Church's service many priests of the caliber and holiness of the Curé of Ars: in our age she has so great a need of them, and she is no less capable of bringing such vocations to full flower.

And we entrust our Priesthood to the Virgin Mary, the Mother of priests, to whom John Mary Vianney ceaselessly had recourse with tender affection and total confidence. This was for him another reason for giving thanks: "Jesus Christ," he said, "having given us all that he could give us, also wishes to make us heirs of what is most precious to him, his holy Mother."[32]

For my part, I assure you once more of my great affection, and, with your Bishop, I send you my Apostolic Blessing.

From the Vatican, 16 March 1986, the Fifth Sunday of Lent, in the eighth year of my Pontificate.

[31]Jn 15:13-15.
[32]Nodet, p.252.

Vocations Support Program

Trinity Communications sponsors a Vocations Support Program designed to help young men with vocations realize their goal of becoming priests. The Program includes six elements, described below.

1. *Fishers of Men: Apostles of the Modern Age*, by John M. Janaro. Profiles of ten priests exemplifying authentic renewal in today's Church. This book is designed to provide the initial inspiration to participate in our program. After reading this book, contact us to receive a copy of number 2, below.

2. *Guidance for Future Priests*, by Fr. Robert J. Fox. This booklet provides an analysis of the authentic vocation, advice on how to pursue a vocation, and a spiritual program for future priests. Free on request. If you're still interested after reading this, contact Trinity to join the Vocations Support Program.

3. *Spiritual Conferences* by Fr. Robert J. Fox. Trinity will send periodic spiritual conferences on cassette to those participating in the program—free of charge.

4. *Youth for Fatima* magazine, edited by Fr. Fox, published by Trinity Communications. Sent free each quarter to all participants in the Program.

5. *Free and reduced-rate books, audio and video cassettes*. Program participants can buy materials for their study and formation at 40% off. Some materials will be provided free as the program unfolds.

6. *Ongoing advice and encouragement.* Keep in touch with us. As we get to know your situation and needs, we'll offer advice and help you make the contacts you need to get into a good pre-seminary program, either in a diocese or a religious order.

Trinity Communications
Jeffrey A. Mirus, President
Fr. Robert J. Fox, Spiritual Advisor
9380 C1 Forestwood Lane
P.O. Box 3610
Manassas, VA 22110
703-369-2429 or 703-369-2789